Golf: A Course in Business

A Few Lessons Golf Can Teach Us About
Management And Entrepreneurship

Maria L. Ellis, MBA

DEDICATION

To all who love the game of golf and the art of business,
may this book be a beacon of guidance and motivation.

ADVANCE PRAISE

"*Golf: A Lesson in Business* is a fascinating exploration of how the challenges and strategies in golf can mirror those in business. This book cleverly intertwines the principles of golf with valuable business lessons, showing how the patience, precision, and strategic thinking required in golf can be applied to the corporate world. Whether you're a seasoned golfer or just curious about the game, this book offers practical advice and fresh perspectives that can be applied both on the course and in your professional life. A compelling read for anyone interested in blending their love of golf with business success."

— Jayant Davar,
Chairman, Sandhar Technologies Ltd. India

"Maria L. Ellis brilliantly captures the essence of how the discipline, strategy, and patience required in golf can be applied to the world of business. *Golf: A Lesson in Business* is a compelling read that offers profound insights and practical advice. Maria's unique perspective and engaging writing style make this book a valuable resource for any entrepreneur or business leader."

— Dr. Antonio Segna,
Manager, Italy

"Maria L. Ellis has skillfully drawn parallels between the strategic world of golf and the dynamic realm of business in *Golf: A Course in Business*. Her insightful analogies and practical advice provide a unique perspective that is both engaging and enlightening. As someone deeply involved in the technological revolution of Bitcoin, I appreciate how Maria emphasizes the importance of strategic planning, adaptability, and resilience—qualities essential in both golf and business. Just as Bitcoin represents a paradigm shift in financial freedom and innovation, Maria's book offers transformative lessons for entrepreneurs striving for success and balance in their professional and personal lives."

— Wences Casares,
Technology Entrepreneur and Bitcoin Advocate, USA

"Mrs. Maria L. Ellis has put together a book that parallels business and golf in a way that takes familiar stories in golf and highlights the preparation, understanding of variables at play and the relationships in business we maintain. I have always enjoyed my time with Maria on the golf course."

— JT Tackett,
Instructor & Director of Fitting
@Georgia Golf Performance, USA

"I read *Golf: A Course in Business* with interest. I was really surprised how many connections Maria L. Ellis was able to find in the course of this game and business. I admire her knowledge of both such different areas and I'm starting to regret that I didn't play golf from a young age (where I could have integrated it with my business)."

— Zdenek Pelc,
Chairman of the Board of Directors, GZ Media

TABLE OF CONTENTS

CHAPTER 1:
HOW CAN I INCREASE SALES AND
PROFITS IN MY BUSINESS?

"Become the person who would attract the results you seek."
— Jim Cathcart

One of my clients, Antonio from Vienna, Austria, is a passionate winemaker. He and his family have a deep love for the art of winemaking. Unfortunately, his business was facing a series of challenges that caused him great anxiety.

For years, Antonio had poured his heart and soul into his vineyard, striving to produce the finest wines. However, despite his best efforts, he found himself facing constant setbacks. Unfavorable weather conditions, pests invading his vineyard, and rising production costs were just a few of the many hurdles facing the winery. These challenges weighed heavily on Antonio's mind, as he feared his lifelong dream of running a successful winery was slipping away.

Amidst the mounting pressure, Antonio found solace in the game of golf. He found that the serene greens and the rhythmic swing of his club provided a much-needed escape from the stresses of his struggling business. Whenever Antonio teed off, he could temporarily set aside his anxieties and immerse himself in the game.

During his golfing escapades, Antonio encountered fellow players who faced similar challenges, like David, a CEO whose company was in the red quarter after quarter, or Jessica, an attorney who struggled to scale her firm. It was through these conversations that he realized the parallels between the game of golf and the challenges he faced in his winemaking business. Golf taught him valuable lessons about resilience, adaptability, and patience.

One sunny afternoon, Antonio found himself in a particularly stressful situation. A sudden hailstorm had ravaged his vineyard, damaging the precious grapevines. The loss seemed insurmountable, and Antonio felt his hopes dwindling. Seeking solace, he headed to the golf course.

As he navigated through the course, Antonio's mind began to clear. With each swing of his club, he channeled his frustration into the game. The game of golf taught him that setbacks were a part of life, and it was his determination to overcome them that mattered the most.

During the round, Antonio struck up a conversation with a seasoned golfer who had faced his fair share of business challenges. The golfer shared his experiences of overcoming adversity and offered valuable advice on how to navigate through difficult times. Inspired by this conversation, Antonio realized that he had to adapt his winemaking strategies and find innovative solutions to the problems he faced.

Returning to his vineyard with a renewed sense of purpose, Antonio implemented changes in his business based on the wisdom he periodically received from his business colleagues at the course. He sought help from experts in pest control, implemented new irrigation techniques to combat adverse weather conditions, and explored cost-effective ways to improve production. Antonio's dedication and newfound resilience began to pay off as his vineyard gradually recovered from the setbacks. As the years went by, Antonio's winery transformed into a thriving business. The once-lost dreams were now a reality, and Antonio's wines gained recognition for their exceptional quality. The game of golf had become not only a source of stress relief for Antonio but also a catalyst for his personal and professional growth.

Antonio's story serves as a testament to the power of finding solace and inspiration outside of one's daily challenges. The game of golf not only provided Antonio with a respite from the anxieties of his business but also offered valuable lessons on perseverance and adaptability. Through the game, Antonio found the strength to overcome the hurdles and turn his struggling winery into a successful business.

One of my goals in writing this book is to explore the parallel histories of business and golf and to distill all of the wisdom I have gained from decades of playing golf and decades as an entrepreneur so you can hit a hole-in-one – in both golf and business.

Early Beginnings: Ancient Trade and Barter Systems

Golf and business both began as simple, localized activities and evolved into structured, global phenomena. They have adapted to technological advancements, expanded internationally, and embraced professionalization and commercialization. Today, both business and golf are integral to the fabric of modern society, influencing culture, driving economic activity, and continuously innovating for a sustainable future.

The concept of business can be traced back to ancient civilizations where bartering systems were used. In Mesopotamia, around 3000 BCE, people exchanged goods and services. Early business practices involved the exchange of commodities like grain, livestock, and crafts.

Similarly, the origins of golf can be traced to ancient times with various stick-and-ball games. The precise beginnings are debated, but like business, golf evolved from simple activities into more structured forms.

Formalization and Rules

As societies developed, so did the complexity of their economic activities. The ancient Greeks and Romans established more formalized trade practices and marketplaces. By the Middle Ages, guilds and chartered companies regulated trade and commerce, laying the groundwork for modern business practices.

In parallel, golf saw its rules and structure formalized in Scotland during the fifteenth century. By the eighteenth century, official rules were established by clubs like the Honorable Company of Edinburgh Golfers, shaping the modern game.

Development and Expansion: Industrial Revolution

The Industrial Revolution of the eighteenth and nineteenth centuries transformed business. The introduction of machinery, factories, and mass production revolutionized how goods were made and distributed. This period saw the rise of major corporations and the foundation of modern economic systems.

During the same period, golf also expanded. The establishment of iconic golf courses and clubs, such as St Andrews, and the standardization of an eighteen-hole round in the 1760s mirrored the industrial growth in business. The sport spread internationally, reflecting the global expansion of business enterprises.

Technological Advancements

The twentieth century brought significant technological advancements, from the telephone and automobile to computers and the internet. These innovations changed how businesses operated, increasing efficiency and creating new industries.

Golf also embraced technology. The introduction of metal clubs, improved golf balls, and modern equipment transformed the game. Television broadcasts and later, the internet, brought golf to a global audience, much like how technology expanded business reach.

Modern Era: Globalization

Today's business landscape is characterized by

globalization. Companies operate across borders, and international trade and investment are crucial to economic growth. The rise of multinational corporations and digital economies exemplifies this global integration.

Golf has similarly globalized. Major tournaments are held worldwide, and players from diverse backgrounds compete at the highest levels. Organizations like the PGA Tour and European Tour have helped globalize the sport, paralleling the expansion of global business networks.

Professionalization and Commercialization

The late twentieth and early twenty-first centuries saw the professionalization of business practices. The rise of business schools, professional certifications, and corporate governance standards improved efficiency and accountability. Businesses became highly specialized and competitive.

Golf saw similar trends with the professionalization of the sport. The establishment of professional tours, endorsement deals, and lucrative prize money transformed golf from a pastime to a professional career. The commercialization of golf, through sponsorships and media rights, mirrors the branding and marketing strategies seen in business.

Cultural Impact and Sustainability: Cultural Significance

Businesses have profoundly impacted culture, shaping lifestyles and societal norms. Brands and corporations influence daily life, driving consumer behavior and societal trends.

Golf, too, has a significant cultural impact. It is a symbol of tradition, sportsmanship, and prestige. Golf courses often serve as social hubs, and the sport is associated with networking and business relations.

Sustainability and Innovation

Modern businesses are increasingly focusing on sustainability and ethical practices. Innovations in green technology and corporate social responsibility initiatives reflect a shift toward more sustainable business models.

Golf is also addressing sustainability. Efforts to reduce the environmental impact of golf courses, such as water conservation and habitat protection, demonstrate the sport's commitment to sustainable practices.

Golf's popularity can be attributed to a combination of factors that appeal to a wide range of people. Here are some key reasons why golf has become such a beloved sport.

Accessibility and Inclusivity

Golf is a sport that can be played by people of all ages and skill levels. From children learning the basics to retirees enjoying a leisurely game, golf offers something for everyone.

Unlike more physically demanding sports, golf is relatively low impact, making it accessible to a broader demographic.

Scenic and Serene Environment

Golf courses are often situated in beautiful landscapes, providing a serene and aesthetically pleasing environment. This aspect of golf appeals to those who enjoy spending time outdoors.

The tranquil setting of a golf course offers a peaceful escape from the hustle and bustle of daily life, making it a perfect activity for relaxation and mental well-being.

Social and Networking Opportunities

Golf is inherently social. Whether playing a round of golf with friends, family, or business associates, it offers ample opportunities for social interaction.

Golf has long been associated with networking, particularly in the business world. The time spent on the course fosters relationship-building in a relaxed, informal setting.

Challenge and Skill Development

Golf is known for its challenging nature. Mastering the game requires a blend of physical skill, strategic thinking, and mental fortitude, which appeals to those who enjoy a complex and rewarding challenge.

The personal nature of the game, where players compete against their previous scores and strive for individual improvement, is a significant draw.

Prestige and Tradition

Golf has a rich history and is steeped in tradition, which adds to its allure. Playing on famous courses and following in the footsteps of legendary golfers holds a special appeal.

High-profile tournaments like The Masters, the U.S. Open, and The Open Championship garner global attention, contributing to the sport's prestige and popularity.

Golf's Relationship with Business and Business Professionals

Golf and business have a symbiotic relationship that has been cultivated over decades. Here's how golf has become intertwined with the business world.

Networking and Relationship Building

The relaxed atmosphere of a golf course provides an ideal setting for business professionals to network and build relationships. Unlike formal meetings, the informal environment of golf facilitates open conversations and rapport-building.

A typical round of golf takes several hours, offering ample time for meaningful interactions. This extended duration is perfect for discussing business matters, negotiating deals, or simply getting to know potential clients and partners better.

Corporate Events and Client Entertainment

Many businesses organize golf tournaments and outings to entertain clients, reward employees, and promote camaraderie. These events often serve as both recreational activities and networking opportunities.

Companies frequently sponsor golf events, using the sport as a platform for brand visibility and corporate hospitality. Sponsoring high-profile tournaments can enhance a company's image and reach.

Skill Development and Personal Traits

The strategic nature of golf, which requires careful planning and decision-making, parallels the strategic skills needed in business. Playing golf can help professionals hone their strategic thinking abilities.

Golf requires patience, discipline, and the ability to stay focused over an extended period – qualities that are equally valuable in the business world.

Shared Interests and Cultural Capital

Golf often serves as common ground for business professionals who share an interest in the sport. This shared interest can be a powerful tool for bonding and creating connections.

In many cultures, being knowledgeable about and proficient in golf can be seen as a mark of prestige and sophistication. This cultural capital can be beneficial in business settings where such traits are valued.

Playing golf can be a great way for business professionals to unwind and relieve stress. Physical exercise, combined with the outdoor environment, contributes to overall well-being.

Engaging in golf provides a balance between work and leisure, promoting a healthier lifestyle which can lead to improved productivity and job satisfaction.

In summary, as a golfer and business owner, I know that golf can benefit a business experiencing challenging financial times. The game imparts lessons in strategic thinking, patience, and honing skills that are smart. The game also teaches discipline and perseverance, essential qualities for a business seeking a breakthrough. If you're looking to grow your business – and improve your golf swing at the same time – keep reading.

CHAPTER 2:
MY EXPERIENCE, BOTH
ON THE GOLF COURSE
AND IN BUSINESS.

"Motivation is the catalyzing ingredient
or every successful innovation."

– Clayton Christensen,
Economist and Harvard Professor

My experience with business and golf started in the summer of 1976. I had just graduated from the University of Massachusetts with an MBA, and my most fervent desire was to work for an international bank in the Corporate Lending Department, offering working capital to Fortune 500 companies located in the Midwest.

I was motivated to obtain my first professional job and start my successful career in banking. I wrote to international banks such as Chase Manhattan Bank, Bank of America, Citibank, and other financial institutions asking for career opportunities. I was lucky to receive employment offers from three banks. I believe that having college work experience and speaking other languages, such as Spanish, helped me in my quest to start an interesting and profitable career in banking.

Quoting one of my Harvard Professor Clayton Christensen's famous quotes, "Motivation is the catalyzing ingredient for every successful innovation," I accepted Bank of

America's job offer and began providing banking services to the bank's existing clients while prospecting for new corporate clients. There was one large corporate client that our International Department coveted, and it was my job to encourage this client to start banking with us. I proceeded to gather as much information as possible for both the corporate office and the company's Chief Financial Officer, who was the decision-maker for this account. My office was located at the Sears Tower in downtown Chicago, and my coveted corporate client was based in Topeka, Kansas. I flew to visit him, he picked me up at the airport, and we had an enjoyable meeting at his office where I presented this corporate client with a $15-million line of credit to finance their international business.

It was only after a few rounds of golf together that this corporate client began to utilize the line of credit and became a profitable client for Bank of America. In retrospect, it took a few rounds of golf to earn his trust. Over the years, I have learned that people prefer to do business with people they like and trust. This is deeply rooted in both psychological comfort and practical efficiency. Trust reduces uncertainty, enhances communication, lowers transaction costs, and fosters long-term relationships. Liking adds a layer of positive social interaction, making business dealings more enjoyable and productive. Together, these factors create a powerful foundation for successful and sustainable business relationships.

People prefer to do business with individuals they like and trust for several compelling reasons that are deeply rooted in human psychology and the practical aspects of building successful business relationships. Trust is a fundamental human need, deeply rooted in psychological foundations. It creates a sense of reliability and predictability, crucial for reducing anxiety and uncertainty. In business, knowing that a partner or client will act consistently, and honor commitments provides a stable environment that fosters confidence. Trust also fosters a sense of safety and security, which is essential for open and honest communication. For instance, when my corporate client and I established mutual trust, he shared important financial information. This transparency enabled us to collaborate effectively and take calculated risks, ultimately enhancing our professional relationship and achieving better outcomes.

Social bonding and rapport are crucial elements in building strong relationships. Positive social interactions release oxytocin, a hormone that promotes bonding and feelings of goodwill. This makes working with individuals we like more pleasant and satisfying.

Emotional resonance also plays a significant role. People naturally gravitate toward those who make them feel good and valued. For instance, after playing a few golf games, our business relationships became more resilient and productive, highlighting the importance of shared positive experiences in fostering strong connections.

Enhanced communication and collaboration are practical business benefits of building trust and rapport. Liking and trust facilitate open dialogue, which is essential for resolving conflicts, negotiating deals, and brainstorming solutions. Effective communication is key to understanding each other's needs and expectations. Efficient collaboration is another advantage. Teams that like and trust each other work together more effectively, leading to better project outcomes and faster problem-solving. Reflecting on my relationship with the CFO from Topeka, several key factors of trust and liking were evident. One particular instance stands out that perfectly exemplifies the power of open dialogue and efficient collaboration. During one of our initial golf games, we found ourselves discussing not just the game but also some of the challenges his company was facing. He opened up about a significant cash flow issue that was impacting their operations. This candid conversation on the golf course facilitated an open dialogue, allowing us to brainstorm potential solutions in a relaxed, informal setting. This experience underscored how trust and rapport can transform casual interactions into opportunities for meaningful collaboration.

Reduced transaction costs are a significant benefit of building trust in business relationships. Trustworthy partners require less oversight, which lowers the need for extensive monitoring and enforcement mechanisms, thereby reducing overall transaction costs. Trust also leads to smoother transactions with fewer disputes and delays. Agreements and contracts are more likely to be honored when parties have mutual trust. In my case with a corporate client, this mutual trust reduced the need for extensive monitoring and enforcement mechanisms, saving both his company and Bank of America on operational costs. This efficiency allowed us to allocate resources more effectively, focusing on strategic growth rather than compliance.

Long-term relationship building is a crucial aspect of business success. Customer loyalty is one of the primary benefits, as clients are more likely to return and do repeat business with individuals and companies they like and trust. This loyalty translates into long-term profitability and stable revenue streams. Referrals and recommendations are another significant advantage. Satisfied clients and partners often refer others to businesses they trust, leading to new opportunities and growth. The trust and rapport we developed on the golf course laid the foundation for a long-lasting and mutually beneficial business relationship. This included not only repeat business but also long-term profitability. For instance, this corporate client initially utilized a $15-million line of credit and later expanded their financial engagements with us to include other banking services such as foreign exchange and cash management.

Risk mitigation is a vital component of successful business relationships. Trustworthy relationships allow for shared risk in ventures, where partners are more likely to support each other through challenges, knowing their counterparts are reliable. Honesty and transparency are also crucial in trusted relationships. Parties are more likely to be open about potential risks and issues, enabling proactive management and mitigation. The trust and rapport we developed on the golf course laid the foundation for effective risk management in our business dealings. For instance, during an economic downturn, the CFO's company faced significant financial challenges that threatened their ability to meet their credit obligations. Because of the strong trust we had built, he approached me openly about their situation. Rather than seeing this as solely their problem, we took a collaborative approach to manage the risk, demonstrating the power of trust in navigating difficult times.

Ethical and cultural dimensions play a significant role in shaping a business's reputation and brand image. A positive reputation for integrity and trustworthiness attracts more clients and partners, serving as a powerful asset in a competitive marketplace. Cultivating a culture of trust and respect within an organization enhances employee morale and productivity, which extends to interactions with external partners. This corporate client often spoke highly of our integrity and trustworthiness at industry events and meetings. His endorsements attracted several new clients who were looking for a reliable and ethical banking partner. These new clients often cited our positive reputation as a key factor in their decision to work with us. In a competitive marketplace, our reputation for integrity became a powerful asset. Prospective clients felt confident in our ability to handle their financial needs ethically and transparently, giving us an edge over competitors who lacked similar endorsements. This trust and positive reputation not only bolstered our client base but also reinforced our commitment to maintaining high ethical standards in all our business dealings.

Ethical standards are a cornerstone of successful business relationships. Liking and trust often stem from shared values and ethical standards. Doing business with like-minded individuals ensures that transactions are conducted in a manner that aligns with one's ethical beliefs. Trustworthy relationships also lead to more socially responsible business practices, as partners are more likely to consider the broader impact of their actions. Our relationship with the CFO's company was highly successful due to our shared commitment to ethical business practices. Early in our interactions, we discovered that we both valued integrity, transparency, and fairness. This alignment of beliefs made our business dealings smooth and mutually respectful. For example, when structuring the $15-million line of credit, both parties prioritized fair terms and conditions. This ensured that the deal was not only profitable but also aligned with our ethical standards. The CFO appreciated our commitment to ethical practices, which reinforced his trust in Bank of America. This shared dedication to ethical conduct solidified our partnership and set a strong foundation for future collaborations.

Psychological and social proof play a crucial role in fostering cognitive ease in business relationships. People find it easier to work with those who provide a sense of familiarity and comfort. Trusted partners reduce mental strain, making business interactions more seamless and comfortable. Positive reinforcement is another key factor. Positive past experiences with a trusted individual reinforce future interactions, creating a cycle of trust and satisfaction. This cycle builds stronger relationships over time. Peer influence is also significant. Seeing others successfully work with a liked and trusted individual provides social proof of their reliability. This peer validation can influence decision-making in favor of trusted partners.

In many industries, reputation networks play a crucial role. Trustworthy individuals and companies are more likely to be recommended and endorsed within these networks. For instance, one of the CFO's business associates, influenced by the CFO's positive endorsement, approached us for a similar line of credit. The endorsement served as a powerful recommendation, highlighting the importance of peer influence in decision-making. This example underscores how reputation and social proof can significantly impact business growth and success.

Golf provided me with a platform to showcase the brand, sponsor tournaments, gaining exposure firsthand. Furthermore, these golf activities offer a retreat from stress, a chance to recharge, reassess, and assess. They can breathe new life and put the business back in fame.

In my experience, both golf players and business owners consider several factors when making decisions. While the specific factors may vary based on the situation, some common considerations include the following.

1. Goals and Objectives

Both golf players and business owners consider their goals and objectives when making decisions. Golf players may have goals such as improving their swing, lowering their handicap, or winning a tournament. Business owners have objectives such as increasing revenue, expanding their customer base, or launching a new product. The decisions they make are guided by these goals and objectives.

2. Data and Information

Both golf players and business owners rely on data and information to inform their decisions. Golf players analyze factors such as course conditions, weather, their performance statistics, and the performance of their competitors. Business owners gather and analyze market research, financial data, customer feedback, and industry trends to make informed decisions about their business strategies.

3. Risk Assessment

Both golf players and business owners assess risks when making decisions. Golf players evaluate the potential risks and rewards of different shots or strategies, considering factors such as the difficulty of the shot, the potential hazards, and the potential for a positive outcome. Business owners assess risks related to market conditions, competition, financial investments, and operational decisions, weighing potential benefits against potential risks.

4. Experience and Expertise

Both golf players and business owners draw on their experience and expertise to make decisions. Golf players rely on their knowledge of the game, their understanding of their strengths and weaknesses, and their familiarity with different strategies and techniques. Business owners use their industry knowledge, understanding of market dynamics, and experience in managing their businesses to make decisions that will drive success.

5. External Factors

Both golf players and business owners consider external factors when making decisions. Golf players take into account factors such as wind direction, course layout, and the behavior of their competitors. Business owners consider factors such as economic conditions, regulatory changes, customer preferences, and industry trends. These external factors influence the decisions they make to adapt to the environment they are operating in.

6. Financial Considerations

Business owners often consider financial factors when making decisions. They assess the financial feasibility of a decision, including costs, potential returns, and the impact on their overall financial health. Golf players may also consider financial factors, such as the cost of equipment or training, when making decisions related to their game.

7. Time Constraints

Both golf players and business owners consider time constraints when making decisions. Golf players must make decisions within a limited timeframe, such as choosing a club and making a shot within a certain time limit. Business owners may have deadlines or time-sensitive opportunities that require them to make decisions quickly.

8. Values and Ethics

Both golf players and business owners consider their values and ethical considerations when making decisions. They consider how their decisions align with their personal or organizational values and the potential impact on stakeholders, such as customers, employees, or the broader community.

Golf players and business owners consider factors such as goals and objectives, data and information, risk assessment, experience and expertise, external factors, financial considerations, time constraints, and values and ethics when making decisions. These factors help them make informed choices that align with their desired outcomes and drive success in their respective fields.

I know that my success in banking was closely interwoven with my fun golf activities that enabled me to bring people together and foster connections. Networking on the green, forging new directions and business deals can be sealed with a friendly game, building relationships, and enhancing the company's name. On the golf course, barriers are broken, walls come down, communication flows freely, and the relaxed atmosphere allows for candid discussions. Golf activities promote teamwork and collaboration.

I will end this chapter by sharing with you a memorable golf story. One crisp autumn morning, I found myself playing golf with another corporate banking client, standing on the eighteenth green, facing a challenging putt that would decide the match. I was standing on the green, facing a sixteen-foot putt with a subtle but significant slope from right to left. The green is fast, making it hard to gauge the speed, and the cup is positioned on a slight incline, increasing the difficulty of the read. As I addressed the ball, I noticed a patch of grain that could affect the ball's roll, demanding an adjustment in your line and stroke. I had to consider the break of the green, aiming several inches to the right to account for the leftward slope. The challenge was compounded by a slight downhill gradient near the hole, requiring me to be gentle with my stroke to avoid overshooting.

With a calm demeanor, I took a few practice swings, visualizing the ball's path. As I made contact, I needed to ensure a smooth, consistent stroke to maintain the ball's intended line and speed. The ball started its journey, curving delicately as it traverses the green, maintaining the perfect pace to nestle into the cup. This difficult putt tested every aspect of my putting game – reading the green, judging the speed, and executing a precise stroke – all while maintaining composure under pressure.

The pressure was immense, but I remembered the advice my mentor once shared: "Trust your instincts, and the path will reveal itself." With a calm breath and steady hands, I made the putt, securing the win. That moment on the green was more than a victory; it was a profound lesson in focus, trust, and perseverance. These are the same principles I now bring to business professionals, helping them navigate the complexities of their careers with the wisdom and Tao of golf. As someone who has experienced firsthand how the game can transform both mindset and strategy, I am uniquely positioned to guide you through this journey. Continue reading this book, and I will share the insights and lessons I have gleaned from countless hours on the course, offering you a fresh perspective on achieving success in business and beyond.

CHAPTER 3:
HOW CAN A GOLFER AND A
BUSINESS OWNER DEFINE SUCCESS?

*"If you are not willing to risk the unusual,
you will have to settle for the ordinary."*
— Jim Rohn

Over the coming chapters, I will teach you what I have learned on the green, and how I have applied it to my businesses.

is about goal setting and motivation. Having measurable goals helps golfers and business owners stay focused and on track by providing clarity, prioritization, action planning, progress monitoring, motivation, course correction, and opportunities for celebration. They create a road map for success and guide their actions and decisions, ensuring that they stay on the path toward achieving their desired outcomes.

Chapter 5 is about the importance of consistency both in business and in the game of golf. Consistency in processes and decision-making ensures reliable data collection, enables effective comparison and benchmarking, helps identify deviations from expected performance, supports continuous improvement, and promotes accountability and transparency. By maintaining consistency, business owners can accurately measure performance and make informed decisions to drive success.

Chapter 6 shows you the importance of building a strong team! Having a diverse team is important in both a golf game and a business. Diversity brings different perspectives, ideas, problem-solving capabilities, creativity, adaptability, customer understanding, and promotes an inclusive work environment. Embracing and leveraging diversity leads to better performance, innovation, and success in both sports and business contexts.

Chapter 7 is about firing fast if your employees are not living the mission and the vision of the company. It helps maintain high standards, preserve team dynamics, maximize efficiency, protect reputation, be cost-effective, and build a strong team. However, it is essential to approach terminations with fairness, empathy, and compliance with legal and ethical considerations.

Chapter 8 is about measuring performance. It emphasizes the importance of focusing on relevant metrics, consistency, course correction, continuous improvement, and having a long-term perspective when measuring performance. By applying these lessons, business owners can effectively track their progress, identify areas for improvement, and make informed decisions to drive success.

Chapter 9 covers mental and emotional factors affecting performance. It's important for both golfers and business owners to recognize and address these factors. Techniques such as visualization, mindfulness, goal setting, seeking support from coaches or mentors, and practicing emotional regulation can help improve mental and emotional well-being, leading to better performance in golf and increased success in business.

Chapter 10 speaks of the important qualities for success. These qualities drive their relentless pursuit of excellence and enable them to make significant contributions in their respective fields.

Chapter 11 explores why golf players and businesses often fail to make the necessary changes to improve the game and increase sales and profits. It's important to note that while these factors may contribute to poor performance and business failure, individual circumstances can vary. Seeking guidance from coaches, mentors, or professionals in the respective fields can help address these factors and improve performance and business outcomes.

Chapter 12 further examines the parallels between golf and business, highlighting lessons learned that could be beneficial. The PGA Tour, widely recognized as the premier professional golf tour in the world, provides valuable insights into leadership, teamwork, and strategic decision-making.

Chapter 13 serves as the conclusion and expresses the author's wish for the reader to be successful in both golf and business.

In summary, the relationship between golf and business is rooted in centuries of tradition and shared values. The principles of golf have evolved while maintaining its core values over time, just like the relationship between golf and business professionals. This book serves as a guide, translating the wisdom of the fairway into actionable insights for the boardroom. I encourage you to focus on implementing the strategies and philosophies shared in your daily business practices, embracing the lessons with dedication and patience, similar to mastering your swing. By integrating these timeless principles, you can enhance your professional acumen and cultivate a balanced approach to business and life.

CHAPTER 4:
GOAL SETTING AND MOTIVATION

"Without goals and plans to reach them, you are like a ship that has set sail with no destination."

— Fitzhugh Dodson

While not all successful business owners are golfers, the principles of the game can be applied to their journeys in remarkable ways. Let's explore how the Tao of golf aligns with the business tactics you'll need through encouraging stories about Tiger Woods, Elon Musk, Jack Nicklaus, Richard Branson and Phil Mickelson. These stories highlight how setting clear goals and staying motivated can lead to remarkable achievements. Here are a few examples of the power of goal setting and motivation.

In the world of professional golf, few names command as much respect and admiration as Tiger Woods. His journey from a young prodigy to one of the most successful golfers in history is a compelling story of the power of setting clear goals and maintaining unwavering motivation.

From a young age, Tiger Woods exhibited a prodigious talent for golf. Born in 1975, Woods was introduced to the game by his father, Earl Woods, who became his first coach and mentor. Earl instilled in Tiger the importance of setting goals and working diligently to achieve them. This lesson would become a cornerstone of Woods' career.

As a teenager, Tiger Woods had already set his sights on greatness. He famously wrote down his goal of winning the

Masters tournament, one of the most prestigious events in golf. This goal was not just a fleeting dream but a tangible objective that he carried with him every day. Woods' relentless focus and dedication to his craft were evident in his rigorous practice routines and mental preparation.

Woods' collegiate career at Stanford University further showcased his exceptional skills and determination. He won numerous amateur titles and quickly transitioned to professional golf, where his impact was immediate. Yet, it was his singular goal of winning the Masters that remained at the forefront of his ambitions.

In 1997, at just twenty-one years old, Tiger Woods achieved what many had deemed impossible. He not only won the Masters but did so in spectacular fashion, with a record-breaking twelve-stroke victory. This historic win not only fulfilled his goal but also marked a new era in the sport. Woods' performance at Augusta National that year became a defining moment in golf history, demonstrating his extraordinary talent and the power of goal setting. Tiger Woods' story is a powerful example of how clear goals and relentless motivation can lead to extraordinary success. His achievement at the Masters was not solely due to his natural talent, but rather the result of years of focused effort, disciplined practice, and an unwavering belief in his abilities. Woods' journey reinforces the importance of having a clear vision and the determination to pursue it, regardless of the obstacles.

For business professionals, Tiger Woods' career offers valuable lessons in perseverance and goal setting. Just as Woods meticulously planned and worked toward his objective, professionals can achieve their aspirations by setting clear, actionable goals and maintaining the motivation to pursue them. His story serves as a reminder that success often requires long-term dedication and an unwavering commitment to one's vision.

Elon Musk is a highly influential and visionary figure in the realms of technology and innovation. His journey from a young entrepreneur to the CEO of groundbreaking companies like SpaceX and Tesla exemplifies the power of setting ambitious goals and maintaining unwavering motivation.

Musk's story begins in South Africa, where he was born in 1971. From a young age, Musk displayed exceptional aptitude for technology and innovation. After moving to the United States, he embarked on a path that would lead to the creation of several pioneering ventures. While he achieved early successes with Zip2 and PayPal, it was his later ventures that truly demonstrated the power of his vision and determination.

Musk's ambition can be seen in his audacious goals for SpaceX and Tesla. With SpaceX, he aimed to revolutionize space travel, making it more affordable and ultimately enabling human colonization of Mars. With Tesla, his goal was to accelerate the world's transition to sustainable energy through electric vehicles and renewable energy products. These goals were not only ambitious but were also considered nearly impossible by many.

The journey was filled with challenges. SpaceX faced numerous technical failures, including several rocket explosions that threatened the company's survival. Tesla also encountered significant hurdles, such as production delays, financial crises, and intense scrutiny from critics and competitors. However, Musk's unwavering determination and resilience kept him and his teams moving forward.

One of Musk's defining traits is his strong sense of purpose. He often speaks about his desire to make a positive impact on the world and to push the boundaries of what is possible. This sense of mission drives him to persist in the face of adversity. Musk's belief in his vision is so strong that he has invested his money into his ventures, even risking personal bankruptcy to ensure their success. In 2008, SpaceX made history as the first privately funded company to send a spacecraft to the International Space Station, demonstrating the viability of private space exploration.

Similarly, Tesla's Model S, launched in 2012, proved that electric cars could rival traditional gasoline vehicles and set a new standard in the automotive industry.

Elon Musk's story is a powerful testament to the impact of setting bold goals and maintaining unwavering motivation. His ability to envision a future that others consider impossible, and his relentless pursuit of that vision, has resulted in transformative innovations that have reshaped industries. Elon Musk plays golf, though he is not known to be an avid golfer in the traditional sense. For Musk, golf serves more as a networking tool than a regular hobby. He recognizes the value of building relationships and making connections on the golf course, often engaging with like-minded individuals and discussing business ideas while playing. Despite his demanding schedule, Musk does make time for golf and even has his personal golf course at his SpaceX facility in Texas. His approach to golf is marked by the same dedication and focus he applies to his business ventures, constantly working on improving his skills on the golf course. For business professionals, Musk's journey offers invaluable lessons in perseverance and visionary thinking. Professionals can apply the same principles by setting ambitious objectives and remaining steadfast in their pursuit, overcoming challenges, and achieving remarkable success.

Jack Nicklaus holds a prominent place in golf history as one of the sport's greatest players. His journey, from a promising young talent to a legendary figure with a record eighteen major championship victories, showcases the power of setting specific goals and employing a meticulous, focused approach to achieve them.

Jack Nicklaus, born in 1940 in Columbus, Ohio, showcased exceptional golfing aptitude from a young age, winning numerous junior titles and establishing himself as a prodigious talent. However, it was his goal-oriented mindset and strategic approach to the game that set Nicklaus apart.

Throughout his career, Nicklaus set both short-term and long-term goals, carefully planning his practice sessions and competitions. He didn't merely aim to win tournaments; he targeted specific areas of improvement in his game. For instance, if he identified weaknesses in his putting or driving, he would dedicate intense focus to those aspects until he saw significant progress. This systematic approach enabled him to continuously refine his skills and stay ahead of the competition.

Nicklaus' long-term goals were equally ambitious. From early on, he aspired to become the greatest golfer in the world, surpassing the records of his idols. This overarching goal provided constant motivation and direction, guiding his decisions and efforts both on and off the course.

A defining moment in Nicklaus' career occurred at the 1962 U.S. Open, where he faced off against the legendary Arnold Palmer in a gripping final round. Nicklaus' composed demeanor, strategic play, and unwavering focus led him to victory, marking his first major championship win. This triumph not only showcased his skill but also his disciplined, goal-oriented approach. Nicklaus' ability to maintain motivation and focus throughout his career spanning over two decades is a testament to his mental fortitude. He consistently set new goals, whether it was improving specific aspects of his game, winning tournaments, or reclaiming the top spot in the rankings. His record-breaking eighteen major championship victories, including six Masters titles, five PGA Championships, four U.S. Opens, and three Open Championships, stand as proof of his relentless pursuit of excellence.

For business professionals, Jack Nicklaus' journey offers valuable lessons in the power of goal-setting and strategic planning. His methodical approach to identifying and addressing weaknesses, setting specific objectives, and maintaining a long-term vision can be applicable in any professional context. Just as Nicklaus systematically worked toward his goals, professionals can achieve remarkable success by setting clear, actionable targets and continuously striving for improvement.

Richard Branson, the dynamic founder of the Virgin Group, embodies the spirit of entrepreneurship with his audacious goals and fearless risk-taking. His journey from a young entrepreneur to a global business magnate is a compelling story of how setting ambitious goals and consistently pushing oneself beyond his or her comfort zone can lead to extraordinary success.

Born in 1950 in Surrey, England, Richard Branson faced challenges with dyslexia, making traditional schooling difficult for him. However, these challenges didn't deter him; instead, they ignited his entrepreneurial spirit. At the age of sixteen, Branson started his first venture, a student magazine that laid the foundation for his future business endeavors.

Branson's ambition was evident from the start. He set lofty goals and fearlessly took risks to achieve them. In 1970, he launched a mail-order record business, which evolved into Virgin Records. Despite lacking formal business training, Branson's innovative approach and willingness to challenge the norms helped him build a successful brand. He made a bold move by signing controversial bands that other labels rejected, a decision that paid off when artists like the Sex Pistols brought massive success to Virgin Records.

One of Branson's most defining characteristics is his determination to venture beyond his comfort zone. In 1984, he boldly entered the highly competitive airline industry with Virgin Atlantic, despite many doubting his ability to compete against established giants like British Airways. However, Branson's unwavering determination and commitment to excellent customer service set Virgin Atlantic apart. Despite facing fierce competition and numerous challenges, his innovative approach revolutionized air travel and established Virgin Atlantic as a major player in the industry. Branson's empire expanded rapidly, encompassing ventures in various sectors, including telecommunications (Virgin Mobile), rail transport (Virgin Trains), and even space travel (Virgin Galactic). Each new venture carried significant risks, but Branson's philosophy of setting high goals and daring to achieve them propelled him forward. His approach involved not merely taking risks, but instead engaging in calculated risk-taking coupled with a strong vision and an unwavering drive to succeed.

Throughout his career, Branson credits much of his success to his ability to set ambitious goals and maintain his motivation. He frequently emphasizes the importance of possessing a strong sense of purpose and the willingness to persevere through adversity. Although his ventures have encountered setbacks and failures, Branson's resilience and capacity for learning from such experiences have been key to his enduring success.

For business professionals, Richard Branson's journey offers invaluable lessons in the power of setting ambitious goals and pushing oneself beyond ones comfort zone. His story demonstrates that achieving success often necessitates taking bold risks and maintaining an unrelenting drive to realize one's vision. Branson's ability to diversify and build a global empire across various industries highlights the significance of innovation, resilience, and a strong entrepreneurial spirit. Like Musk, Richard Branson enjoys playing golf and sees it as a recreational activity that fits well with his adventurous spirit. Branson uses golf not just for leisure but also as an opportunity to network and build relationships in a relaxed environment. His involvement in various adventurous and competitive activities, including golf, reflects his dynamic and multifaceted personality.

Phil Mickelson is renowned not only for his incredible skill but also for his tenacity and competitiveness. His journey from a talented amateur to a multiple major championship winner is a powerful testament to the importance of setting both short-term and long-term goals. Mickelson's dedication to these goals has played a crucial role in his enduring success in golf.

Born in 1970 in San Diego, California, Phil Mickelson, often affectionately referred to as "Lefty" due to his left-handed swing, demonstrated a natural aptitude for golf from a young age. Encouraged by his father, Mickelson honed his skills through countless hours of practice and competition. His early achievements in amateur golf, including winning the U.S. Amateur title and NCAA championships, set the stage for his professional career.

What distinguishes Mickelson is his unyielding focus on goal-setting. He has always believed that having specific targets is essential for maintaining motivation and concentration. Throughout his career, Mickelson has set both short-term goals, such as improving aspects of his game, and long-term goals, such as winning major championships. This structured approach has served as a cornerstone of his success.

One of Mickelson's most notable achievements occurred in 2004 when he won his first major championship at the Masters. This victory was the culmination of years of dedication and goal-setting. Despite being one of the top players in the world, Mickelson had faced significant pressure and scrutiny for his inability to secure a major win. However, his perseverance paid off when he sank an eighteen-foot birdie putt on the final hole, securing the coveted green jacket. This victory was not only a personal triumph but also a validation of his goal-oriented approach.

Mickelson's commitment to goal setting did not stop with his first major win. He continued to set new targets, consistently pushing himself to achieve more. Over the years, he went on to win multiple major championships, including the PGA Championship and The Open Championship. Each victory was a result of meticulous planning, hard work, and unwavering determination to achieve the goals he had set for himself.

One of the most remarkable aspects of Mickelson's career is his ability to sustain a high level of performance over several decades. Even as he aged, Mickelson remained proactive in setting new goals, adapting his game, and staying competitive. In 2021, at the age of fifty, he made history by becoming the oldest player to win a major championship with his victory at the PGA Championship. This unprecedented achievement showcased his tenacity and the effectiveness of his goal-setting strategy.

Mickelson's story serves as a powerful example of how setting clear goals can drive success. His ability to remain focused and motivated, despite facing challenges and setbacks, underscores the importance of having a structured approach to achieving one's ambitions. For business professionals, Mickelson's journey offers valuable lessons in the power of goal setting. By establishing specific, actionable goals and maintaining an unwavering drive to achieve them, individuals can overcome obstacles and reach new heights in their careers.

The mentioned successful entrepreneurs and professional golfers serve as examples from the worlds of business and golf, designed to aid you in setting and achieving your goals. These stories highlight the significance of goal setting and motivation in both professional golf and entrepreneurship. They demonstrate that setting specific goals, staying motivated, and being willing to take risks can lead to incredible achievements and success. Goal setting and motivation are crucial in both a golf game and running a profitable business for several reasons.

Clarity of Direction

Setting clear goals provides a sense of direction and purpose. In golf, specific goals like improving swing mechanics, reducing handicap, or winning a tournament help golfers focus their efforts and prioritize their training and practice sessions. Similarly, in business, goals such as increasing revenue, expanding into new markets, or improving customer satisfaction provide a clear road map for business owners to follow and guide their decision-making process.

Focus and Commitment

Establishing objectives is crucial for both golfers and business owners to maintain focus and dedication. In golf, pursuing a specific target, such as winning a championship, keeps players motivated and committed to their training regimen. Similarly, in business, defining clear goals helps owners and their teams concentrate on key priorities, allocate resources effectively, and make strategic decisions aligned with these objectives.

Measurement of Progress

Setting clear targets provides benchmarks for measuring progress and success. In golf, monitoring progress toward goals like reducing handicap or enhancing accuracy enables golfers to evaluate their performance and pinpoint areas for improvement. In business, establishing measurable objectives, such as boosting sales revenue or hitting a profit margin target, allows business owners to track their progress and adjust strategies as needed.

Motivation and Drive

Having distinct goals fuels motivation and drive. For golfers, aiming for achievements such as winning a tournament or reaching a personal best score ignites the determination to put in the necessary effort and overcome challenges. In business, setting ambitious and meaningful objectives can inspire owners and their teams to push boundaries, innovate, and strive for exceptional results.

Accountability and Responsibility

Defined goals foster a sense of accountability and responsibility. In golf, setting targets holds players accountable for their performance and development, encouraging proactive improvement. Similarly, in business, goal-setting cultivates a culture of accountability, where individuals and teams take ownership of their actions and work toward the organization's shared objectives.

Continuous Improvement

Establishing goals drives ongoing improvement and growth. In golf, setting progressive targets allows players to continually challenge themselves, learn from experiences, and develop new skills and strategies. In business, goal-setting promotes the pursuit of innovative solutions, investment in professional development, and adaptation to changing market conditions, fostering business growth and profitability.

Setting specific targets offers clarity and focus on what needs to be achieved. By defining precise objectives, both golfers and business owners can determine what they are aiming for, such as improving swing mechanics or boosting sales revenue. This specificity helps channel their efforts and resources toward the actions needed to reach those objectives.

Progress Tracking

Golfers and business owners can monitor their performance over time, identifying areas for improvement and adjusting strategies or techniques accordingly. Regularly tracking progress ensures they stay on course and make informed decisions to optimize their performance or business operations.

Motivation and Accountability

Clear, measurable goals serve as a powerful source of motivation and accountability. With specific targets to work toward, golfers and business owners experience a sense of purpose and drive. Observing their progress and accomplishments fuels their determination to keep pushing forward. Additionally, these goals hold individuals and teams accountable, as progress can be objectively measured against the set targets.

Effective Planning and Resource Allocation

Defining measurable goals aids in effective planning and resource allocation. Golfers and business owners can break down their goals into smaller, actionable steps. This approach allows for the creation of realistic plans and efficient allocation of resources such as time, energy, and finances. Prioritizing activities that directly contribute to achieving these goals helps optimize efforts and resources.

Decision-Making and Strategy Development

Having clear, measurable goals provides a solid foundation for decision-making and strategy development. Golfers and business owners can make informed decisions about the actions and strategies needed to reach their targets. These goals guide resource allocation, determine priorities, and assess the effectiveness of different approaches, enabling strategic decisions that align with their desired outcomes.

Continuous Improvement

By setting specific and measurable targets, golfers and business owners can identify areas where they can improve. They can analyze data and feedback to identify patterns, strengths, and weaknesses. This information can then be used to refine their techniques, processes, or business strategies, driving ongoing growth and improvement.

Overall, having measurable goals in both golf and business provides clarity, progress tracking, motivation, accountability, effective planning, informed decision-making, and opportunities for continuous improvement. It allows golfers and business owners to set clear targets, monitor their progress, make data-driven decisions, and optimize their efforts toward achieving success.

Measurable goals help golfers and business owners stay focused and on track in the following ways.

Clarity of Direction

Defining specific targets provides a clear direction and purpose. Golfers and business owners understand exactly what they are working toward and what needs to be achieved. This clarity ensures they stay focused on the actions and milestones necessary to reach their objectives.

Prioritization of Efforts

Setting measurable goals allows individuals to prioritize their efforts effectively. By identifying key activities and tasks that directly contribute to their goals, golfers and business owners can allocate their time, energy, and resources accordingly, avoiding distractions from less important activities.

Action Planning

With specific targets in mind, golfers and business owners can develop detailed action plans. These plans break down goals into actionable steps and create a structured road map for success, outlining necessary tasks and timelines to keep them on track.

Progress Monitoring

Establishing measurable goals facilitates regular progress monitoring and tracking. This process enables golfers and business owners to measure their performance against set targets, assess any gaps, and make adjustments as needed, fostering accountability and keeping them on course.

Motivation and Inspiration

Clearly defined goals act as a source of motivation and inspiration. Seeing tangible progress as they move closer to their targets boosts the confidence of golfers and business owners, inspiring them to continue pushing forward even during challenging times.

Course Correction

The ability to measure progress against goals allows for timely course correction. If current strategies or actions are not yielding the desired results, golfers and business owners can make necessary adjustments. This flexibility ensures they stay aligned with their objectives.

Celebrating Milestones

Overall, measurable goals help golfers and business owners stay focused and on track by providing clarity, prioritization, action planning, progress monitoring, motivation, course correction, and opportunities for celebration. They create a road map for success and guide their actions and decisions, ensuring that they stay on the path toward achieving their desired outcomes.

By applying these principles, you too can harness the power of ambitious goal-setting and fearless perseverance to overcome challenges and reach new heights in your personal and professional life. Let these stories shared with you in this chapter, inspire you to think big, take risks, and pursue your goals with unwavering determination.

CHAPTER 5:
HOW IMPORTANT IS CONSISTENCY, BOTH ON AND OFF THE COURSE?

"Small disciplines repeated with consistency every day lead to great achievements gained slowly over time." Success is usually not instant; it is a journey. One step at a time! So, choose a routine or habits that you can maintain, and then build on it."

– John Maxwell

Tiger Woods is one of the most successful professional golfers in history. Throughout his career, Woods has emphasized the importance of consistency in his game. He believes that consistently executing the fundamentals of golf, such as a solid swing and precise putting, is crucial for success. Woods' dedication to consistency has allowed him to achieve a remarkable record, including fifteen major championship victories.

Mental toughness and visualization were essential components of Woods' success – and necessary components to business, as well. Woods understood the power of the mind in shaping performance and utilized techniques such as visualization to mentally rehearse shots and visualize success. By picturing himself executing flawless shots, he was able to build confidence and maintain a positive mindset on the course.

His ability to stay focused and composed in high-pressure situations set him apart from his competitors. He possessed a deep reservoir of mental toughness, allowing him to perform at his best when the stakes were highest. This mental resilience was evident in his numerous comeback victories and ability to thrive under intense scrutiny.

In addition to his on-course achievements, Woods made a significant impact through his philanthropic efforts. His foundation, the Tiger Woods Foundation, has been instrumental in providing educational opportunities and support for underserved youth. Through initiatives like the Tiger Woods Learning Centers and scholarships, Woods has shown his commitment to making a positive difference in the lives of others.

Tiger Woods' success is a testament to the power of consistency, dedication, and a growth mindset. His unwavering commitment to excellence, both on and off the golf course, has made him an iconic figure in the world of sports. Woods' story serves as an inspiration to aspiring athletes and anyone striving for greatness: with consistent effort, disciplined practice, and a strong belief in oneself, extraordinary success is within reach. Another critical component of Woods' routine was mental training. He worked extensively on developing mental toughness, which he considered essential for maintaining focus and composure under pressure. Woods practiced visualization techniques, mentally rehearsing his shots and envisioning successful outcomes. This practice helped him build confidence and stay mentally sharp during competitions.

Woods also employed mindfulness and meditation techniques to manage stress and maintain a positive mindset. His ability to stay calm and focused, even in high-stakes situations, was a testament to his mental discipline.

Tiger Woods was meticulous about setting both short-term and long-term goals. He broke down his ultimate objectives into manageable, incremental goals, which he pursued with determination. After each practice session or tournament, Woods would evaluate his performance, identifying areas for improvement. This continuous cycle of goal setting, self-assessment, and refinement enabled him to make steady progress.

Woods' approach to goal setting was not just about winning tournaments but also about personal growth and mastery of the game. By constantly challenging himself and striving for improvement, he maintained his motivation and drive. Woods' philosophy of consistent practice extended beyond the physical aspects of golf. He was a voracious learner, studying the techniques and strategies of other great golfers, as well as seeking advice from coaches and mentors. His openness to learning and adapting his game was a significant factor in his sustained success.

Finally, Woods understood the importance of reflection and adaptation. He regularly took time to reflect on his performances, both successes and failures. This reflective practice allowed him to learn from his experiences and make necessary adjustments to his training and strategies. Woods' ability to adapt and evolve his game was crucial in maintaining his competitive edge over the years.

Tiger Woods' path to greatness is a powerful illustration of how small disciplines, repeated with consistency every day, lead to monumental achievements over time. His daily routines and habits – focused practice, physical fitness, mental training, goal setting, continuous learning, and reflection – formed the bedrock of his success. For business professionals, Woods' approach offers valuable lessons in the power of consistent, incremental progress. By adopting similar disciplines and maintaining a relentless focus on improvement, you too can achieve remarkable success, one step at a time.

Warren Buffett is known to play golf, though it is not a primary hobby of his. He owns golf clubs and is a member of Augusta National, one of the most prestigious golf clubs in the world. However, golfing is more of an occasional activity for him rather than a regular pastime. He has participated in charity golf events and enjoys the social and networking opportunities that come with the sport Buffett's golf clubs were even auctioned off, indicating his participation in the sport, although he may not be as avid a golfer as some of his contemporaries, Warren Buffett, known as the "Oracle of Omaha," is widely regarded as one of the most successful investors and business owners in the world. Born in 1930 in Omaha, Nebraska, Buffett exhibited a knack for business and investing from a young age. His early ventures included selling chewing gum, Coca-Cola, and weekly magazines door-to-door. By the age of eleven, he made his first stock purchase, marking the beginning of an illustrious investment career.

Buffett's investment philosophy revolves around the importance of consistency. This principle has been the bedrock of his approach, guiding him through the tumultuous waters of the stock market for decades. He believes in investing in companies with consistent earnings and long-term growth potential, avoiding the temptation to chase short-term gains. Instead, Buffett's strategy is to buy and hold quality companies, allowing them to grow over time. This patient and disciplined approach has proven to be extraordinarily successful.

One of the cornerstones of Buffett's philosophy is his focus on businesses with strong fundamentals. He looks for companies with solid management, competitive advantages, and a history of profitability. By sticking to these criteria, he ensures that his investments are grounded in sound principles rather than speculative whims. This commitment to consistency has allowed him to build a substantial fortune and become one of the wealthiest individuals globally.

Buffett's company, Berkshire Hathaway, is a testament to his consistent investment approach. Originally a struggling textile company, Berkshire Hathaway has grown into a diversified conglomerate under Buffett's leadership. He has acquired and nurtured a wide range of businesses, from insurance companies like GEICO to iconic brands like Coca-Cola and Apple. Each of these investments aligns with his philosophy of long-term value creation.

But Buffett's commitment to consistency extends beyond his professional life. He emphasizes the importance of consistency in personal habits and decision-making as well. Buffett is known for his disciplined lifestyle, which includes maintaining a modest diet, a simple routine, and a strong work ethic. He often speaks about the value of habits, quoting Aristotle: "We are what we repeatedly do. Excellence, then, is not an act, but a habit."

Buffett's personal life reflects his investment principles. He avoids impulsive decisions and maintains a steady course, focusing on long-term goals rather than short-term pleasures. This discipline has allowed him to remain grounded despite his immense wealth and success. In addition to his investment prowess, Buffett is also a renowned philanthropist. He has pledged to give away most of his fortune through the Giving Pledge, a commitment he co-founded with Bill and Melinda Gates. This initiative encourages the world's wealthiest individuals to donate a significant portion of their wealth to charitable causes. Buffett's philanthropy is another manifestation of his consistent values, emphasizing the importance of giving back to society.

Warren Buffett's life and career are a testament to the power of consistency. His unwavering commitment to his investment principles has not only made him one of the richest individuals in the world but also a respected figure in both the financial and philanthropic communities. By emphasizing consistency in both his professional and personal life, Buffett has built a legacy that extends far beyond his financial success, inspiring countless individuals to pursue excellence through disciplined, long-term thinking.

Both Tiger Woods and Warren Buffett believe that consistency in their respective fields brings several benefits. Here are some of the key benefits they associate with consistency.

Improved Performance

Both Woods and Buffett believe that consistency leads to improved performance. In golf, Tiger Woods emphasizes that consistently executing the fundamental aspects of the game, such as a consistent swing and precise putting, leads to better results on the course. Similarly, Warren Buffett believes that consistently following his investment principles and sticking to a long-term approach leads to better investment performance over time.

Trust and Reputation

Consistency builds trust and a strong reputation in their fields. Tiger Woods' consistent performance and success in golf have earned him the trust and admiration of fans, fellow golfers, and sponsors. Warren Buffett's consistent investment track record has established him as a trusted and respected figure in the world of finance. Both individuals have built a reputation for excellence through their consistent efforts.

Long-Term Success

Both Woods and Buffett understand the importance of long-term success. They believe that consistency is a key factor in achieving sustained success. In golf, Woods' consistent dedication to practice and improvement has allowed him to achieve numerous victories and major championships over his career. Buffett's consistent investment approach has enabled him to build a substantial fortune and become one of the most successful investors in history.

Adaptability and Learning

Consistency also allows for adaptability and continuous learning. Tiger Woods constantly fine-tunes his game and adapts to different courses and playing conditions while staying true to his consistent approach. Warren Buffett consistently learns from his investment mistakes and adapts his strategies accordingly. Both individuals embrace consistency as a foundation for ongoing growth and improvement.

Reduced Stress and Decision-Making Clarity

Consistency reduces stress and decision-making

complexity. By having consistent routines and approaches, both Woods and Buffett can eliminate unnecessary distractions and focus on what matters most. This clarity leads to better decision-making and overall performance.

By recognizing the benefits of consistency, Tiger Woods and Warren Buffett have achieved remarkable success in their respective fields. Their belief in the power of consistency serves as a valuable lesson for aspiring professionals and business owners. Consistency in playing golf and in business is essential for success. Here is an example of how I apply consistency to both golf and business. I have always been passionate about two things: golf and business. As a real estate investment advisor working for a global real estate company, I often find myself comparing the principles of success in both arenas. I believe that consistency is the cornerstone of excellence, whether on the golf course or in my real estate business. As often as I can, I head to the golf course; I love trying different golf courses around the world. I love the tranquility of the early hours, the dew on the grass, and the challenge of the game. But more than anything, I appreciate how golf mirrors the demands of my professional life. Each swing, each putt, and each hole require focus, precision, and a consistent approach.

I remember my early days learning to play golf. I was inconsistent, often changing my grip, my stance, and my swing. My game was erratic, and my scores reflected it. Then I met Coach JT, a seasoned golfer who taught me the importance of consistency. "Maria," Coach JT said, "golf isn't just about power or speed. It's about maintaining a steady form, a reliable swing, and a calm mind. It's about doing the same thing, the right way, every time." Under Coach JT's guidance, I began to see improvement. I developed a routine: the same warm-up exercises, the same practice drills, and the same mental preparation before each game. My swing became more reliable, my putts more accurate, and my overall game more consistent. This steady progress led to lower scores and a deeper enjoyment of the game. At work, I apply the same principles. In the fast-paced real estate industry, it is easy to get caught up in the latest trends and make impulsive decisions. But I know that long-term success depends on a consistent strategy. Just as in golf, where a consistent swing leads to better results, in business, a consistent approach leads to sustainable growth.

Last spring, while playing a round of golf with my friends in Phuket, Thailand, I shared my thoughts on consistency. "You know," I said, "golf has taught me so much about business. It's not about the big wins or the dramatic shots. It's about the small, consistent actions that add up over time. Every swing, every putt, every decision we make, both on the course and in the office, contributes to our overall success." My friends nodded in agreement, reflecting on how their steady efforts had led to their achievements. They realized that the same principles applied to their work: maintaining focus, following through on commitments, and continuously improving their skills. As we finished our golf game, I felt a deep sense of satisfaction. I had mastered the art of consistency in both my passions. My golf game was better than ever, and my real estate business continued to be fun and profitable. I now know that the key to my success is not a secret formula or a stroke of luck but the power of consistent effort, day in and day out.

In the end, I know that whether on the golf course or in business, consistency is essential. It is the steady hand that guides the swing, the reliable business plan that drives the real estate business forward, and the unwavering commitment to excellence that defines my life. Through consistency, I have achieved success, and I know that this principle will continue to guide me in all my future endeavors.

In both golf and business, consistency breeds confidence, reliability, and trust. It allows individuals and organizations to establish a track record of success and build a reputation for excellence. Whether on the golf course or in the business world, practicing consistency is key to achieving long-term success. Consistency in processes and decision-making is crucial for accurately measuring performance in golf and in business. Here's how it helps.

Reliable Data

Consistency ensures that data collection processes are standardized and reliable. When processes are consistent, the data gathered is more accurate and consistent as well. This reliability of data allows for meaningful analysis and measurement of performance indicators. Inconsistent processes may lead to skewed or unreliable data, making it difficult to accurately measure performance.

Comparison and Benchmarking

Consistency in processes allows for effective comparison and benchmarking. When processes and measurement methods remain consistent over time, you can compare performance data from different periods and identify trends. This helps in setting benchmarks, understanding performance fluctuations, and making informed decisions based on reliable comparisons.

Identifying Deviations

Consistency in decision-making helps in identifying deviations from expected performance. When decision-making processes are consistent, it becomes easier to trace the impact of decisions on performance outcomes. If there are significant deviations from expected results, consistent decision-making allows for a systematic evaluation of the decisions made, enabling you to pinpoint areas that require improvement.

Continuous Improvement

Consistency in processes and decision-making supports a culture of continuous improvement. By measuring performance consistently, you can identify areas that need improvement and implement changes systematically. Consistency allows you to track the impact of these changes over time, enabling you to make data-driven decisions to optimize performance.

Accountability and Transparency

Consistency in processes and decision-making promotes accountability and transparency within the organization. When processes are consistent, it is easier to hold individuals and teams accountable for their performance. Consistent decision-making ensures that decisions are made based on objective criteria and not influenced by personal biases or preferences, fostering transparency in the measurement of performance.

In summary, consistency in processes and decision-making ensures reliable data collection, enables effective comparison and benchmarking, helps identify deviations from expected performance, supports continuous improvement, and promotes accountability and transparency. By maintaining consistency, business owners can accurately measure performance and make informed decisions to drive success.

CHAPTER 6:
WHY IS BUILDING A STRONG TEAM IMPORTANT TO THE SUCCESS OF THE GOLFER AND THE ENTREPRENEUR?

"Coming together is a beginning, staying together is progress, and working together is success."

– Henry Ford

Two examples of professional golfers and successful entrepreneurs who believe in the importance of building a strong team for their success in both the short and long term, and how they are building a long-term legacy, are Phil Mickelson and Greg Norman.

Phil Mickelson, known as "Lefty," is a highly accomplished professional golfer and successful entrepreneur. He understands the significance of building a strong team to support his career and business endeavors. Here's how he is building a long-term legacy.

Mickelson recognizes that success is not achieved alone. He has surrounded himself with a team of experts, including coaches, trainers, caddies, and business advisors. Mickelson values their expertise and relies on their support to enhance his golf performance and make strategic business decisions.

Mickelson emphasizes collaboration and trust within his team. He believes in open communication, sharing ideas, and seeking input from his team members. By fostering a collaborative environment, Mickelson can leverage the diverse skills and perspectives of his team to improve his game and make informed business choices.

To secure long-term success and build a legacy, Mickelson invests in the development of his team. He provides resources and opportunities for his team members to grow and excel in their respective roles. This investment not only benefits his career but also creates a positive environment that fosters loyalty and commitment among his team members.

Mickelson believes in giving back to the golfing community and mentoring young talent. He actively supports junior golf programs, sponsors scholarships, and provides mentorship to aspiring golfers. By nurturing and inspiring the next generation, Mickelson aims to leave a lasting legacy in the sport.

Greg Norman, also known as "The Great White Shark," is a legendary professional golfer and successful entrepreneur. He recognizes the importance of building a strong team to achieve success and create a long-term legacy. Here's how he approaches it.

Norman understands the value of diversity within his team. He believes that bringing together individuals with different skill sets, backgrounds, and perspectives leads to innovative thinking and better decision-making. Norman seeks out experts from various fields to support his business ventures and contribute to his long-term success.

Norman's entrepreneurial spirit is reflected in his team-building approach. He surrounds himself with individuals who share his vision and passion for business. He collaborates with professionals who have expertise in areas such as finance, marketing, and brand development to build successful ventures beyond the golf course.

One way Norman is building a long-term legacy is through golf course design. He has established a renowned reputation as a golf course architect, creating stunning and challenging courses worldwide. Norman's designs not only leave a physical legacy but also provide enjoyment and inspiration for golfers for generations to come.

Norman's long-term legacy also extends to his philanthropic and environmental efforts. He actively supports charitable causes and environmental initiatives. Through his philanthropy, he aims to make a positive impact on society and leave a lasting legacy of giving back.

Both Phil Mickelson and Greg Norman understand that building a strong team is crucial for success in their careers and the longevity of their legacies. By leveraging the expertise of their teams, collaborating, mentoring, and making a positive impact beyond their individual achievements, they are creating a lasting influence in the world of golf and entrepreneurship.

Greg Norman contributes to his long-term legacy through his golf course designs in several ways.

Creating Memorable Experiences

Greg Norman's golf course designs are known for their unique and memorable experiences. He incorporates natural landscapes, strategic challenges, and stunning aesthetics to create courses that golfers will remember for a lifetime. By designing courses that leave a lasting impression, Norman ensures that his legacy as a golf course architect will be cherished by golf enthusiasts for generations to come.

Challenging Golfers

Norman's designs are renowned for their strategic and challenging layouts. He carefully considers factors such as course topography, wind patterns, hazards, and green undulations to create courses that require skill, precision, and strategic thinking. By providing golfers with a challenging yet enjoyable experience, Norman's designs become a testament to his dedication to the sport and his commitment to pushing the boundaries of golf course architecture. Environmental Sustainability: Greg Norman is committed to environmental stewardship in his golf course designs. He integrates sustainable practices, such as water conservation, native plantings, and wildlife preservation, into his designs. By prioritizing environmental sustainability, Norman ensures that his courses have a minimal impact on the surrounding ecosystems and can be enjoyed by future generations without compromising the environment.

Legacy of Innovation

Norman's golf course designs often showcase innovative concepts and technologies. He embraces advancements in golf course architecture, such as incorporating modern drainage systems, state-of-the-art irrigation technologies, and innovative bunker designs. By pushing the boundaries of design and embracing innovation, Norman's courses become a testament to his forward-thinking approach and contribute to his long-term legacy as a pioneer in the field.

Inspiring Future Architects

Norman's designs serve as an inspiration for aspiring golf course architects. His innovative and visually appealing layouts set a high standard for future designers to aspire to. By showcasing his creativity and expertise, Norman encourages the next generation of golf course architects to push the boundaries of design and leave a lasting legacies in the industry.

Through his golf course designs, Greg Norman not only creates exceptional golfing experiences but also leaves a legacy as a visionary golf course architect. His commitment to creating memorable experiences, challenging golfers, promoting environmental sustainability, embracing innovation, and inspiring future architects ensures that his impact on the world of golf will endure for years to come.

Building a strong team is important for both a golfer and an entrepreneur because it can significantly contribute to their success.

For instance, my friend Wayne relies on a team of professionals, including a caddy, coach, and support staff, to optimize his performance. His caddy assists with course strategy, club selection, and reading greens, providing valuable insights and guidance. Wayne's coach helps analyze and improve his swing, technique, and mental game. His support staff handles logistics, equipment, and other administrative tasks. By building a strong team, Wayne can leverage the expertise and support of these individuals, enabling him to focus on the game and make better decisions. The collective efforts of the team help Wayne achieve better results and increase chances of success.

My Harvard classmate and successful entrepreneur, Christine, who lives in Australia, has created a strong team, including some talented family members. Building a strong team of skilled individuals with complementary expertise is crucial for the continued success of the business. Her team includes co-founders, employees, advisors, and mentors. Each member brings unique skills, knowledge, and perspectives to the table, contributing to the overall success of the business. A strong team helps with tasks such as product development, marketing, operations, finance, and customer service. They provide support, guidance, and accountability, helping Christine navigate obstacles and make informed decisions. By building a strong team, she has leveraged the collective strengths of her team members, resulting in a more productive and successful business.

In both scenarios, building a strong team enhances collaboration, communication, and problem-solving capabilities. Ultimately, a strong team can help both the golfer and the entrepreneur achieve their goals and reach higher levels of success.

Surrounding yourself with knowledgeable people is crucial in both a golf game and running a successful business because having the right team can significantly impact your performance and outcomes. Here's why.

Expertise and Specialization

Knowledgeable individuals bring expertise and specialization to the table. In a golf game, having a coach or caddy who understands the intricacies of the sport can provide valuable insights, guidance, and strategies to improve your skills and performance. Similarly, in business, having team members with expertise in areas such as finance, marketing, operations, or sales can contribute to making informed decisions, implementing effective strategies, and overcoming challenges.

Diverse Perspectives

Surrounding yourself with knowledgeable people brings diverse perspectives to the table. In golf, different viewpoints from experienced players or coaches can help you identify weaknesses, discover new techniques, and find innovative solutions to improve your game. In business, a diverse team can offer fresh ideas, alternative viewpoints, and different approaches to problem-solving, leading to more creative and effective solutions.

Collaborative Learning

Being surrounded by knowledgeable individuals creates an environment of collaborative learning. In golf, learning from experienced players or coaches allows you to acquire new skills, techniques, and strategies that can enhance your game. In business, working with a team of knowledgeable individuals fosters a culture of continuous learning and development, where team members can share their knowledge, learn from each other's experiences, and collectively improve their skills and expertise.

Support and Accountability

Having the right team provides support and accountability. In golf, a team of knowledgeable individuals can provide encouragement, motivation, and constructive feedback, helping you stay focused, motivated, and accountable for your performance. In business, a supportive team can provide guidance, advice, and feedback, holding each other accountable for individual and collective goals. They can also provide emotional support during challenging times, boosting morale and resilience.

Complementary Skills

Surrounding yourself with knowledgeable people allows

you to leverage their complementary skills. In golf, having a team that includes individuals with different strengths, such as long drives, accurate putting, or strategic thinking, can create a well-rounded approach to the game. In business, having a team with diverse skills and expertise enables you to leverage each team member's strengths, delegate tasks effectively, and achieve optimal results.

Networking and Connections

Knowledgeable individuals often have extensive networks and connections. In golf, being connected to experienced players, coaches, or sponsors can open doors to opportunities, sponsorships, or collaborations that can enhance your game. In business, having a team with strong networks can provide access to potential clients, partnerships, investors, or mentors, expanding your business's reach and opportunities for growth.

The right team brings expertise, diverse perspectives, collaborative learning, support, accountability, complementary skills, and networking opportunities. They can significantly enhance your performance, decision-making, problem-solving, and overall success. Building a strong and knowledgeable team is a key factor in achieving your goals and maximizing your potential.

Having a diverse team is important in both a golf game and a business because diversity brings a range of benefits and advantages that contribute to better performance, innovation, and success. Here's why diversity matters.

Different Perspectives and Ideas

A diverse team brings together individuals with different backgrounds, experiences, and perspectives. In a golf game, having players from various skill levels, playing styles, and cultural backgrounds can provide different approaches to the game, strategies, and techniques. In a business, diversity in terms of gender, race, age, ethnicity, and socioeconomic background can bring fresh ideas, alternative viewpoints, and innovative solutions to challenges.

Enhanced Problem-Solving and Decision-Making.

Diversity in a team leads to enhanced problem-solving and decision-making. In golf, diverse perspectives can help identify weaknesses, uncover new strategies, and find innovative ways to improve performance. In a business, diverse teams are more likely to consider a wider range of options, challenge assumptions, and make better-informed decisions. Different viewpoints can lead to more thorough analysis, reduced biases, and improved outcomes.

Creativity and Innovation

A diverse team fosters creativity and innovation. In golf, players with different playing styles and approaches can inspire each other, leading to the development of new techniques or game strategies. In a business, diverse teams bring a variety of experiences, knowledge, and insights that can fuel creativity and spark innovation. Different perspectives can generate fresh ideas, identify untapped market opportunities, and drive product or service innovation.

Improved Problem-Solving and Adaptability

Diversity in a team enhances problem-solving skills and adaptability. In golf, exposure to different playing conditions, courses, and opponents helps players adapt their game and develop versatile skills. In a business, a diverse team can bring a range of problem-solving approaches, adaptability to change, and resilience. By drawing on diverse experiences and skills, teams can navigate challenges, find creative solutions, and adapt to dynamic market conditions more effectively.

Better Customer Understanding and Market Reach

Diversity in a team improves customer understanding and expands market reach. In golf, understanding and appreciating the diverse backgrounds and preferences of players and fans can help tailor experiences, events, and marketing efforts to reach a wider audience. In a business, a diverse team can provide insights into different customer segments, cultural nuances, and market preferences, enabling more effective marketing, product development, and customer satisfaction.

Inclusive and Positive Work Environment

A diverse team promotes an inclusive and positive work environment. In golf, embracing diversity fosters a sense of belonging, respect, and camaraderie among players from different backgrounds. In a business, diversity promotes a culture of inclusion, equal opportunities, and diversity of thought. A positive work environment leads to higher employee engagement, increased productivity, and improved overall performance.

In summary, having a diverse team is important in both a golf game and a business. Diversity brings different perspectives, ideas, problem-solving capabilities, creativity, adaptability, customer understanding, and promotes an inclusive work environment. Embracing and leveraging diversity leads to better performance, innovation, and success in both sports and business contexts.

CHAPTER 7:
THE PRINCIPLE OF FIRE FAST AND HIRE SLOWLY CAN BE IMPORTANT IN BOTH A GOLF CAREER AND RUNNING A BUSINESS

*"Firing employees, unfortunately,
that's a part of doing business."*
– Paul Wolfowitz

John sat in his office, staring at the performance reports in front of him. He had just wrapped up a challenging meeting with his senior management team about the latest struggles of one of their key business units. It was clear that the unit's leader, Mark, was underperforming, and the negative impact on the team was undeniable. John knew it was time to make a difficult decision. He recalled the advice his mentor had given him years ago: "Fire fast, hire slow."

Reflecting on this principle, John remembered a business client story that had left a profound impact on him. Years ago, his mentor, Sarah, a seasoned CEO, had shared an experience from her career. Sarah had taken over a struggling company with a history of poor leadership decisions. The previous CEO had been hesitant to make tough calls, leading to a culture of complacency and inefficiency.

Sarah's first major decision was to let go of several underperforming executives who had been with the company for years. It wasn't easy, but she understood that their prolonged inefficiency was costing the company dearly. By firing fast, Sarah sent a clear message: performance and accountability were non-negotiable.

Next, Sarah took her time to hire replacements. She sought individuals who not only had the right skills but also aligned with the company's values and vision. This careful selection process was time-consuming, but the results spoke for themselves. The new team brought fresh energy, innovative ideas, and a commitment to excellence. The company's performance improved dramatically, setting the stage for sustained growth and success.

John knew that he needed to apply the same principle to his current situation. Holding onto Mark any longer would only drag the team down further. It was time to make a change, even though it was a tough decision. After making the call, John felt a mix of relief and resolve. He now turned his attention to finding the right person to lead the team. He was determined to hire slowly, ensuring that the new leader would be a perfect fit for the company's culture and long-term goals.

As John considered these principles, he couldn't help but draw parallels to his passion for golf. On the golf course, consistency and patience were crucial, just as they were in business. He thought about the lessons he had learned from his experiences and those of other successful golfers. One vivid example comes to mind: a fellow golfer named David. David had been struggling with his game for years, constantly changing his equipment, coaches, and even his swing technique in search of a quick fix. However, these impulsive decisions only made his game more erratic. David's turning point came when he decided to fire his coach, who had been providing inconsistent advice, and took the time to find a coach who truly understood his strengths and weaknesses.

David's new coach, Emily, emphasized the importance of a consistent approach. She spent months analyzing David's swing, understanding his style, and building a tailored training regimen. The progress was slow but steady. Over time, David's game improved significantly, and he became one of the most reliable players in his league. By firing fast and hiring slow, David had transformed his performance on the course.

John saw another parallel in his friend Lisa, a professional golfer who had built a successful career through meticulous planning and consistency. Lisa never rushed into decisions, whether it was choosing a new club or adjusting her training routine. She understood that quick fixes rarely led to lasting results. Instead, she focused on incremental improvements, always maintaining a steady course. Her disciplined approach paid off, making her one of the top golfers in the country.

Back in his office, John felt a renewed sense of clarity. The principles of firing fast and hiring slow, combined with the importance of consistency, were essential not only in business but also in life. Just like in golf, where each swing and putt required focus and precision, in business, each decision had to be made thoughtfully and strategically.

As he prepared to meet his team to discuss the next steps, John felt confident in his approach. He knew that by embracing these principles, he could steer his company toward greater success, just as he had improved his golf game. Whether on the course or in the boardroom, the power of consistency and the wisdom of making the right decisions at the right time were undeniable keys to excellence.

Here are some stories of professional golfers and successful business owners who believe in the principle of "firing fast and hiring slow"

Arnold Palmer, a legendary golfer and successful businessman, was renowned for his strong work ethic and meticulous attention to detail. He understood that success, both on the golf course and in business, required making tough decisions and building a reliable team. Palmer firmly believed in the principle of "firing fast and hiring slow," which played a crucial role in his achievements. In his golf career, Palmer was known for his aggressive style and decisive actions. He carried these traits into his business ventures, understanding the importance of addressing performance or behavior issues promptly. Palmer knew that keeping an underperforming employee could harm the morale and productivity of the entire team. By making quick decisions to fire, when necessary, he ensured that his organization remained dynamic and efficient.

One notable example of Palmer's adherence to this principle was during the early days of his business empire, which included the successful Arnold Palmer Enterprises and his golf course design company. When Palmer noticed that an employee was not meeting expectations or was a poor cultural fit, he didn't hesitate to make the tough call. This approach prevented prolonged periods of inefficiency and kept his teams focused and motivated.

However, Palmer's decisiveness in firing was balanced by his careful and deliberate approach to hiring. He understood that bringing the right people on board was essential to maintaining the high standards he set for his businesses. Palmer took his time to ensure that new hires were not only skilled but also aligned with his vision and values. This thorough vetting process helped him build a team of dedicated and capable individuals who contributed to the success of his ventures.

One of the most significant examples of Palmer's success due to his hiring strategy was his collaboration with IMG, the sports management company. Palmer's partnership with IMG founder Mark McCormack was built on mutual respect and shared values. This careful selection of business partners and associates helped Palmer create a robust and enduring brand that extended beyond his golfing career.

By adhering to the principle of "firing fast and hiring slow," Palmer was able to build a successful brand and leave a legacy both on and off the golf course. His approach ensured that his businesses were staffed with the right people, maintaining a high level of performance, and fostering a positive work environment. This philosophy not only contributed to his professional success but also inspired countless others to apply the same principles in their careers.

Arnold Palmer's legacy is a testament to the power of making quick, decisive actions when necessary and taking the time to build a team that truly fits the organization's needs. His life and career continue to serve as an example of how the principles of "firing fast and hiring slow" can lead to enduring success.

Phil Mickelson, a highly accomplished golfer and successful entrepreneur, has carved out a notable career by adhering to a strategic approach both on and off the golf course. Known for his keen decision-making skills and business acumen, Mickelson firmly believes in the principle of "firing fast and hiring slow." This philosophy has significantly contributed to his success, enabling him to build and maintain high-performing teams in his business ventures.

Mickelson's approach to handling performance issues is both swift and decisive. He understands that holding onto underperforming employees can be detrimental to progress and growth. For Mickelson, it is crucial to address these issues promptly to maintain the overall health and efficiency of his organization. By making quick decisions to let go of employees who are not meeting expectations, Mickelson ensures that his teams remain dynamic and focused.

An example of Mickelson's adherence to this principle can be seen in his management of his business ventures, such as his golf course design company. When he identifies an employee who is not contributing effectively or aligning with the company's goals, he does not hesitate to take action. This approach minimizes disruptions and helps maintain a high standard of performance across his businesses.

On the flip side, Mickelson takes a deliberate and meticulous approach to hiring new talent. He recognizes the importance of finding individuals who not only possess the necessary skills but also share the same values and mindset as his businesses. This careful selection process ensures that new hires are a good fit for the company culture and can contribute positively to the team's long-term goals. Mickelson's thorough vetting process might involve multiple interviews, background checks, and assessments to ensure that the candidates are truly aligned with his vision.

One of the most notable instances of Mickelson's successful application of this principle was during the formation of his management team for his various business endeavors. By taking his time to hire the right people, Mickelson has been able to build a team that supports his ambitions and contributes to the growth and success of his ventures. This deliberate approach to hiring has allowed him to avoid the pitfalls of rushing the process and ending up with employees who do not fit well within the organization.

By following the principle of "firing fast and hiring slow," Phil Mickelson has been able to build a successful career both in golf and in business. His ability to take quick, decisive actions when necessary and his commitment to carefully selecting new team members have enabled him to maintain high standards and achieve sustained success. Mickelson's strategic approach serves as an inspiration to others, demonstrating how thoughtful decision-making and a focus on long-term goals can lead to excellence in any field. Greg Norman, a former professional golfer and highly successful entrepreneur, is renowned for his aggressive and decisive approach to business. Known as the "Great White Shark," Norman's philosophy of "firing fast and hiring slow" has been a cornerstone of his business strategy, enabling him to build a lucrative business empire alongside his illustrious golfing career.

Norman's decisive nature is evident in how he addresses performance or behavior issues within his organizations. He understands that lingering too long on poor performance or bad behavior can negatively impact the overall success and morale of the business. By swiftly addressing these issues, Norman ensures that his teams remain efficient and focused. This approach prevents the spread of negativity and keeps the organization moving forward without unnecessary delays.

A specific example of Norman's application of this principle can be seen in his leadership of Great White Shark Enterprises, a diversified company with interests in everything from golf course design to clothing lines. When an employee fails to meet expectations or disrupts the team dynamic, Norman does not hesitate to make the necessary changes. This quick action helps maintain a high level of performance and sets a standard for accountability within the organization.

However, Norman's aggressive approach to addressing performance issues is balanced by his meticulous and patient strategy for hiring new talent. He believes in thoroughly vetting candidates to ensure they are the right fit for his business ventures. This process involves multiple interviews, background checks, and assessments to confirm that the candidates possess the skills, values, and mindset necessary for long-term success within the company.

One notable instance of Norman's thorough hiring process was during the expansion of his golf course design business. Recognizing the importance of having a team that shared his vision and standards, Norman took the time to carefully select architects and designers who not only had the technical skills but also aligned with his philosophy and business goals. This deliberate approach to hiring has allowed Norman to build a team that consistently delivers high-quality work, contributing to the global success of his golf course design business.

By adhering to the principle of "firing fast and hiring slow," Greg Norman has been able to create a successful and diverse business empire. His ability to take quick, decisive actions when necessary and his commitment to carefully selecting new team members have enabled him to maintain high standards and achieve sustained success. Norman's strategic approach serves as an inspiration to others, demonstrating how thoughtful decision-making and a focus on long-term goals can lead to excellence in both sports and business.

Preserving Team Dynamics

By hiring slowly and carefully evaluating candidates, you can ensure that each team member aligns with the goals, values, and work ethic of the golf career or business. This reduces the likelihood of conflicts and miscommunications that can negatively impact team dynamics. Making the difficult decision to part ways swiftly with individuals who do not fit in can help maintain a strong and cohesive team.

Driving Success

Choosing the right team members is crucial for achieving success in both a golf career and running a business. By hiring slowly and thoroughly evaluating candidates, you increase the likelihood of finding individuals with the necessary skills and experience to contribute to the overall goals of the golf career or business. Making the difficult decision to let go of underperforming or incompatible individuals ensures that the team remains high-performing and focused on driving success.

In summary, the principle of "fire fast and hire slowly" is important in both a golf career and running a business. By being selective and deliberate in the hiring process, individuals can build strong and cohesive teams that contribute to their overall success. Firing fast allows for the prompt resolution of conflicts or issues within the team. In both golf and business, having a harmonious and cohesive team is vital for success. If a team member is disruptive, unmotivated, or not aligned with the team's goals and values, it may be necessary to make a quick decision to preserve the overall dynamics and morale of the team.

Maximizing Efficiency

Firing fast and removing underperforming or ill-suited individuals from your team allows you to optimize efficiency. In golf, it ensures that you have the right caddy, coach, or support staff who can contribute to your development and success. In business, it means having employees who are competent, motivated, and aligned with the company's vision and goals. By hiring slowly, you take the time to carefully evaluate candidates and select those who are the best fit for the role, minimizing the need for future terminations.

Protecting Reputation

Firing fast can help protect your reputation and brand, both in golf and business. If a team member's actions or behavior reflect negatively on you or your organization, it is important to take swift action to mitigate any damage to your reputation. By addressing issues promptly, you demonstrate your commitment to professionalism, integrity, and accountability.

Cost-Effectiveness

Firing fast and hiring slowly can be cost-effective in the long run. In golf, investing time, effort, and resources in a coach or support staff who are not delivering results can hinder your progress and waste valuable resources. Similarly, in business, hiring the wrong people can lead to productivity losses, increased turnover, and additional recruitment and training costs. Taking the time to carefully evaluate candidates before hiring can help minimize these costs.

Building a Strong Team

Hiring slowly allows you to be thorough in your candidate selection process, ensuring you find the best fit for your team. In both golf and business, building a strong team is crucial to achieving success. By carefully selecting individuals who possess the right skills, experience, attitude, and cultural fit, you increase the likelihood of creating a high-performing team that can contribute to your goals and objectives.

Promptly addressing performance or behavior issues in

a golf career or running a business is important for several reasons.

Maintaining a Competitive Edge

In a golf career, addressing performance or behavior issues promptly allows you to maintain a competitive edge. By recognizing and addressing areas of improvement or problematic behavior early on, you can take the necessary steps to enhance your skills, refine your technique, and stay ahead of your competition. Similarly, in business, addressing performance issues ensures that your team is operating at its best, delivering high-quality products or services, and staying ahead of competitors.

Personal Growth and Development

Addressing performance or behavior issues is crucial when it comes to both a golf career and running a business. By acknowledging areas that need improvement and taking action to address them, individuals can enhance their skills, knowledge, and expertise in golf. In a business setting, addressing performance issues provides opportunities for employees to receive feedback, training, or coaching, thus enabling them to grow and develop professionally.

Promptly resolving issues is crucial for maintaining positive team dynamics and collaboration. In golf, addressing problems such as communication breakdowns, conflicts, or lack of cooperation within a team fosters a harmonious and supportive environment. Similarly, in business, addressing performance or conduct issues ensures effective teamwork, promotes collaboration, and creates a cohesive team atmosphere.

Identifying and resolving obstacles allows individuals to enhance their performance and achieve better results. By tackling challenges that hinder progress, golfers can improve their game. In business, addressing performance issues ensures that employees have the necessary resources, skills, and support to deliver optimal results. Addressing performance or behavior issues also demonstrates professionalism and integrity. It shows that individuals are committed to upholding high standards in both a golf career and a business setting. By addressing issues promptly, individuals uphold their personal values, the integrity of the game, or the reputation of their business.

On the other hand, ignoring performance or behavior issues can have negative consequences and lead to escalation. In a golf career, unresolved issues can impact an individual's game and hinder their progress, which can result in frustration or disappointment. Similarly, in a business, unaddressed performance issues can affect team morale, productivity, and ultimately, the success of the organization. Promptly addressing these issues helps prevent them from escalating and causing more significant negative impacts.

In conclusion, promptly addressing performance or behavior issues in a golf career or running a business is crucial for maintaining a competitive edge, promoting personal growth and development, fostering positive team dynamics, enhancing performance and results, maintaining professionalism and integrity, and avoiding escalation or negative impacts. It is important to address these issues with fairness, empathy, and a focus on constructive solutions..

CHAPTER 8:
MEASURING PERFORMANCE

"A business absolutely devoted to service will have only one worry about profits. They will be embarrassingly large."

— Henry Ford

By integrating performance measures and strategies, businesses can gain a comprehensive understanding of their operations, make informed decisions, and achieve sustained success. Here are some examples of how successful entrepreneurs and avid golfers measure performance.

James Mitchell, a successful entrepreneur and golfer, was known for his rigorous approach to measuring performance in both his business ventures and on the golf course. James firmly believed that consistent tracking and analysis of performance metrics were crucial to achieving sustained success.

In his early twenties, James founded TechInnovate, a startup focused on developing cutting-edge software solutions for the tech industry. He quickly realized that measuring performance was essential to drive growth and improve efficiency. James implemented a comprehensive performance measurement system within his company. This system included key performance indicators (KPIs) that tracked everything from sales growth and customer satisfaction to employee productivity and project timelines.

Every month, James held review meetings with his team to analyze these metrics. He believed that regular assessment and feedback were critical to identifying areas of improvement and ensuring that the company stayed on track with its goals. For instance, if a particular product was not meeting sales targets, James and his team would dive deep into the data to understand the reasons behind the shortfall and develop strategies to address the issues. This data-driven approach enabled TechInnovate to consistently outperform its competitors and achieve significant market share.

James's commitment to performance measurement extended to his passion for golf. As an amateur golfer aiming to improve his game, he applied the same principles that had brought him success in business. James used a variety of performance measurement methods to track his progress on the golf course. He recorded detailed statistics for every round he played, including fairways hit, greens in regulation, putts per round, and sand saves.

To gain deeper insights, James also invested in advanced golf technology, such as launch monitors and swing analysis software. These tools provided him with precise data on his swing mechanics, ball flight, and club performance. By analyzing this data, James could identify specific areas where he needed to improve, such as his driving accuracy or putting consistency.

James's dedication to measuring performance in golf paid off. Over the years, his handicap steadily decreased, and he started winning local tournaments. His analytical approach allowed him to make informed adjustments to his training regimen and equipment, leading to continuous improvement in his game.

The parallels between James's success in business and golf were clear. In both domains, he relied on systematic measurement and analysis to drive performance. This disciplined approach not only helped him achieve his goals but also inspired those around him. Employees at TechInnovate admired James's commitment to excellence and adopted similar practices in their work, leading to a culture of continuous improvement within the company.

One particular instance of James's dual application of performance measurement stood out. During a critical phase of product development at TechInnovate, James noticed that the team was struggling to meet deadlines. He decided to apply a technique from his golf training to the business context: breaking down complex tasks into smaller, measurable components. By doing so, the team could track their progress more effectively and address issues as they arose.

This strategy proved to be a game-changer. The project was completed on time, and the product launch was a resounding success. James's ability to transfer his performance measurement skills from the golf course to the business world demonstrated the power of this approach.

James Mitchell's story exemplifies how a commitment to measuring performance can lead to success in multiple areas of life. Whether in the boardroom or on the fairway, his meticulous approach to tracking and analyzing metrics enabled him to achieve excellence and inspire others to do the same. Samantha Turner, another example of a successful entrepreneur and accomplished amateur golfer, exemplifies the use of performance measurement methods to excel in both her business and golf pursuits. As the founder and CEO of GreenTech Innovations, a French company specializing in sustainable energy solutions, Samantha's analytical mindset and attention to detail have propelled her to the top of her industry.

Samantha's journey began when she noticed a gap in the market for affordable and efficient solar energy products. With an engineering background, she set out to develop innovative solutions to address this need. Early on, Samantha recognized the importance of measuring performance to ensure her company's success. She established a comprehensive system to track various metrics, including production efficiency, sales growth, customer satisfaction, and environmental impact.

Every quarter, Samantha conducted detailed performance reviews with her management team. These reviews focused on analyzing key performance indicators (KPIs) to identify strengths, weaknesses, and opportunities for improvement. By maintaining a rigorous approach to performance measurement, GreenTech Innovations consistently delivered high-quality products and services, earning a reputation as a leader in the sustainable energy sector.

Samantha's commitment to performance measurement extended beyond her business. As a passionate golfer, she applied the same principles to improve her game. Samantha meticulously tracked her golf performance, keeping detailed records of each round, including fairways hit, greens in regulation, putting averages, and sand saves. This data-driven approach allowed her to identify patterns and areas for improvement.

To further enhance her performance, Samantha utilized advanced golf technology, such as GPS devices and swing analysis apps, to gain deeper insights into her game. By analyzing this data, she could make informed adjustments to her technique and strategy. For example, if Samantha noticed a recurring issue with her short game, she would dedicate extra practice time to chipping and putting, using targeted drills to address specific weaknesses.

One of Samantha's noteworthy achievements came during a regional golf tournament where she faced tough competition. By relying on her performance data, she developed a strategic game plan that played to her strengths and minimized her weaknesses. Her meticulous preparation paid off, and she won the tournament, attributing her success to the detailed analysis and consistent practice regimen.

Samantha's ability to apply performance measurement techniques in both her business and golf endeavors has been fundamental to her success. At GreenTech Innovations, her data-driven approach fosters a culture of continuous improvement and innovation. In golf, it has helped her refine her skills and achieve competitive success. Samantha often shares her philosophy with aspiring entrepreneurs and golf-ers, emphasizing the importance of tracking performance and making data-driven decisions. She believes that success in any field requires a commitment to excellence and a willingness to continuously analyze and improve.

Her story demonstrates that whether in the boardroom or on the golf course, the principles of performance measurement are universal. By maintaining a rigorous approach to tracking and analyzing metrics, Samantha Turner has built a thriving business and become a formidable competitor in the world of golf, exemplifying the power of this disciplined approach.

When measuring business performance, consider the following benchmarks:

1. **Sales and Revenue:** For instance, Henry Ford closely monitored sales and revenue to assess the company's performance. He tracked the number of cars sold, market share, and overall revenue. Ford aimed to increase sales and revenue by producing affordable and desirable automobiles.

2. **Customer Satisfaction:** Ford recognized the importance of customer satisfaction. He believed that satisfied customers would lead to repeat business and positive word-of-mouth.

3. **Feedback and Reviews:** Ford measured performance by gathering customer feedback and reviews, aiming to continually improve the product and customer experience.

4. **Production Efficiency, Quality Control, and Cost Reduction:** These are some of the ways Henry Ford measured performance in his automotive business. His focus on production efficiency, quality control, cost reduction, sales, customer satisfaction, and employee productivity contributed to the success of Ford Motor Company.

Phil Mickelson, a highly accomplished golfer and successful entrepreneur, has long been known for his meticulous approach to measuring performance. Both on the golf course and in his business ventures, Mickelson combines quantitative and qualitative factors to ensure consistent improvement and success.

On the golf course, Mickelson tracks traditional statistics such as driving accuracy, greens in regulation, and putting average. These metrics provide a clear picture of his technical performance and highlight areas where he can improve. For instance, if his driving accuracy declines, Mickelson might focus more on his tee shots during practice sessions. If his putting average increases, he might spend additional time on the green, working on his short game? However, Mickelson goes beyond these standard metrics by also evaluating his mental and emotional performance. He understands that golf is as much a mental game as it is a physical one. To this end, Mickelson measures his ability to stay focused, manage pressure, and make strategic decisions during tournaments. He often reflects on his mental state during crucial moments, analyzing how well he maintained concentration and composure under pressure. This self-awareness allows him to identify mental strategies that work and those that need adjustment.

One memorable example of Mickelson's holistic approach to performance measurement was during the 2013 Open Championship at Muirfield. Facing challenging conditions, Mickelson not only relied on his technical skills but also demonstrated exceptional mental resilience and strategic thinking. His ability to stay calm and make smart decisions under pressure played a significant role in his victory, underscoring the importance of mental and emotional performance in achieving success.

In his business ventures, Mickelson applies a similar blend of quantitative and qualitative performance metrics. He tracks financial metrics such as revenue growth, profit margins, and return on investment to ensure his businesses are financially healthy. These quantitative measures provide a clear picture of the company's performance and help identify areas for improvement.

Customer satisfaction is another critical metric for Mickelson. He regularly reviews feedback from customers, looking for patterns and insights that can guide product development and service improvements. By prioritizing customer satisfaction, Mickelson ensures that his businesses meet or exceed customer expectations, which is essential for long-term success.

Innovation and adaptability are also key performance indicators for Mickelson. In the rapidly changing business landscape, staying ahead of the competition requires continuous innovation and the ability to adapt to new market conditions. Mickelson measures his businesses' performance in these areas by tracking the development of new products and services, as well as their ability to respond to market trends and customer needs.

For instance, Mickelson's approach to his wine business, Mickelson Wines, exemplifies his commitment to innovation and quality. He closely monitors market trends and customer preferences, ensuring that his wines not only meet high standards of quality but also align with consumer tastes. This attention to detail and willingness to adapt have contributed to the success of his wine brand. By focusing on both quantitative and qualitative performance metrics, Phil Mickelson has built a successful career in golf and business. His ability to comprehensively measure and analyze his performance allows him to make informed decisions, continuously improve, and maintain a competitive edge. Mickelson's story serves as an inspiration, demonstrating how a balanced approach to performance measurement can lead to sustained success in any field.

Greg Norman, a former professional golfer and highly successful entrepreneur, has always approached both his golfing and business endeavors with a strategic mindset, emphasizing performance measurement through a blend of financial metrics and strategic goals.

In his business career, Norman sets clear objectives related to revenue growth, profitability, and market share. He meticulously tracks financial statements, cash flow, and key performance indicators (KPIs) to assess the overall health and success of his ventures. For instance, in his company Great White Shark Enterprises, which includes diverse interests such as golf course design, real estate, and clothing lines, Norman uses detailed financial metrics to drive decision-making.

One example of Norman's strategic approach to business can be seen in his wine business, Greg Norman Estates. Here, he sets specific revenue targets and closely monitors market share within the competitive wine industry. Norman uses financial reports and market analysis to identify trends, optimize operations, and ensure profitability. His attention to financial metrics has allowed Greg Norman Estates to grow steadily, earning a reputation for high-quality wines.

Additionally, Norman emphasizes strategic goals beyond just financial success. He aims to build a brand that stands for excellence, quality, and innovation. He continuously seeks opportunities for expansion and diversification, always with an eye on long-term sustainability and market leadership. This strategic vision is supported by regular performance reviews and adjustments to business plans based on the latest data and market conditions.

On the golf course, Norman's approach to measuring performance is equally rigorous. He evaluates his performance based on tournament results, consistency in scoring, and his ability to perform under pressure. Norman's career, which includes ninety-one international tournament victories, two Open Championships, and numerous top finishes in major championships, demonstrates his commitment to excellence.

Norman tracks his consistency by analyzing his scoring patterns across different tournaments. He looks at his ability to maintain low scores and minimize mistakes, focusing on areas that need improvement. For example, if his putting accuracy is lower than desired, Norman dedicates more practice time to this aspect of his game, using statistical analysis to guide his training efforts. Moreover, Norman understands the importance of mental toughness in golf. He measures his performance under pressure by reflecting on how well he handles critical moments in tournaments. This introspection helps him develop strategies to improve his mental game, ensuring he remains composed and focused during high-stakes situations.

Beyond the technical aspects of performance, Norman places a strong emphasis on maintaining a positive and professional image both on and off the course. He believes that a golfer's reputation can significantly impact their career and opportunities. Norman has always conducted himself with professionalism, earning respect and admiration from peers and fans alike.

In business, this commitment to a positive image translates into how he manages his companies and interacts with stakeholders. Norman ensures that his businesses operate with integrity, high ethical standards, and a customer-centric approach. By doing so, he builds trust and loyalty, which are crucial for long-term success.

Greg Norman's ability to measure performance through a combination of financial metrics and strategic goals has been instrumental in his success as both a golfer and an entrepreneur. By setting clear objectives, monitoring key indicators, and maintaining a positive image, Norman has built a legacy of excellence that continues to inspire others in both the sports and business worlds. His story exemplifies how disciplined performance measurement and strategic thinking can lead to sustained success across diverse fields.

Annika Sorenstam, one of the most successful female golfers in history, is renowned for her holistic approach to measuring performance. Her method encompasses not only traditional golf statistics but also physical fitness, mental preparation, and personal growth. Sorenstam meticulously tracks her golf performance through various statistics. She measures driving distance, accuracy, and putting average to get a clear picture of her technical skills. By analyzing these metrics, Sorenstam identifies areas of her game that need improvement. For instance, if her driving accuracy declines, she focuses on refining her swing technique and consistency off the tee. Similarly, if her putting average increases, she dedicates more time to practicing on the greens. Sorenstam understands that physical fitness plays a crucial role in her performance on the golf course. She incorporates a rigorous fitness regimen into her training routine, which includes strength training, cardiovascular exercises, and flexibility workouts. This commitment to physical fitness not only enhances her stamina and power but also reduces the risk of injuries. Sorenstam's dedication to maintaining peak physical condition has been a significant factor in her sustained success over the years.

Mental clarity and emotional resilience are central to Sorenstam's approach to performance measurement. She believes that the mental aspect of golf is just as important as the physical. Sorenstam practices mindfulness and meditation to improve her focus and concentration during tournaments. She also works with sports psychologists to develop strategies for managing pressure and staying calm under stress. By cultivating a strong mental game, Sorenstam ensures that she can perform at her best, even in high-stakes situations.

Sorenstam takes a holistic view of her overall well-being, understanding that physical health, mental clarity, and emotional resilience are interconnected. She pays close attention to her diet, ensuring she fuels her body with nutritious foods that support her energy levels and recovery. Sorenstam also prioritizes rest and recovery, recognizing the importance of sleep and relaxation in maintaining peak performance.

Beyond her golf career, Sorenstam sets goals related to personal growth and development. She is passionate about expanding her knowledge and skills in the business world. After retiring from professional golf, Sorenstam launched several successful ventures, including the Annika Academy, a golf school designed to help players of all levels improve their game, and the Annika Foundation, which supports aspiring female golfers. Sorenstam continuously seeks opportunities for learning and growth, whether through furthering her education, attending business seminars, or mentoring young athletes.

Sorenstam's holistic approach to measuring performance has not only made her one of the most successful golfers in history but also a role model for athletes worldwide. Her emphasis on overall well-being, mental strength, and continuous personal development has set a new standard in the world of sports. Sorenstam's legacy extends beyond her impressive achievements on the golf course; she has inspired countless individuals to pursue excellence in all aspects of their lives.

Through her story, Annika Sorenstam demonstrates that true success comes from a balanced approach that values physical health, mental fortitude, and a commitment to lifelong learning. Her holistic performance measurement method is a testament to the power of integrating various facets of life to achieve sustained excellence. Refers to the average number of putts a golfer takes to complete a round. It is a measure of a golfer's ability to make accurate putts and convert strokes into successful holes.

In running a business, performance can also be measured using a range of quantitative and qualitative factors, such as.

Revenue: This metric measures the total income generated by the business over a specific period. It reflects the effectiveness of sales and marketing efforts, as well as the overall financial health of the business.

Profit Margin: Profit margin is a measure of the profitability of the business and represents the percentage of revenue that is retained as profit after deducting expenses. It indicates the efficiency and effectiveness of the business's operations.

Customer Satisfaction: This qualitative factor assesses the level of satisfaction and loyalty among customers. It can be measured through customer surveys, feedback, and reviews, and reflects the quality of products or services provided by the business.

Employee Productivity: This metric measures the output and efficiency of employees in completing their tasks and responsibilities. It can be measured through factors such as sales targets achieved, projects completed, or customer interactions.

By using a combination of these quantitative and qualitative performance measures, both professional golfers and successful business owners can track their progress, set goals, and continually strive for improvement in their respective fields.

This metric measures the average number of putts a golfer takes to complete a round. It reflects the golfer's proficiency in putting and can indicate their overall performance on the greens.

In running a business, performance can be measured using various metrics, depending on the specific goals and objectives of the business. Here are a few common performance metrics.

My business partner Steve measures revenue as the total income generated by our business from its primary operations. It is a fundamental measure of business performance and indicates the effectiveness of sales and marketing efforts. On a monthly basis, we measure the profit margin of our business by calculating the percentage of net income relative to revenue. A higher profit margin indicates better financial performance and efficiency in managing costs. We also measure customer satisfaction through annual surveys, feedback, and reviews. It reflects the quality of our services, customer experience, and overall performance in meeting customer expectations. Employee productivity is another important measure, and we assess it through various metrics like sales per employee, units produced per hour, or customer service response time. Higher employee productivity often indicates better business performance. Our most important measure is the Return on Investment (ROI): ROI measures the return generated from an investment relative to its cost. It is commonly used to evaluate the performance of marketing campaigns, projects, or investments in assets. A higher ROI indicates better performance and efficiency in generating returns.

Every month, Steve meticulously tracked the revenue generated by Innovate Solutions. Revenue, the total income from the company's primary operations, served as a fundamental measure of their business performance. By analyzing revenue trends, they could gauge the effectiveness of their sales and marketing efforts. He is also focused on the profit margin, which they calculated by determining the percentage of net income relative to revenue. A higher profit margin indicated better financial performance and efficiency in managing costs. On a monthly basis, Steve would dive into the financial reports, scrutinizing costs and identifying areas where they could improve efficiency. By focusing on these key performance metrics, Steve can build a thriving business. Their approach ensured that they could make informed decisions, identify areas for improvement, and celebrate their successes.

These are just a few examples of how performance can be measured in golf and business. The specific metrics used may vary depending on individual circumstances and goals.

A game of golf can teach a business owner several valuable lessons about measuring performance. Here are a few lessons that can be applied to business.

In golf, understanding the trade-off between distance and accuracy is important for on-course strategy. For example, deciding whether to hit a driver or a four-metal off the tee. Driving accounts for 28 percent of the best pros' scoring advantage, and putting counts for about 15 percent. The question is, how much of the remaining 57 percent is due to approaching shots and how much is due to the short game. Golfing legend Ben Hogan once said that the three most important scoring clubs, in order, are the driver, the putter, and the wedge.

In business and golf, we measure performance using the following data.

Focus on Metrics

In golf, players focus on metrics such as score, fairways hit, greens in regulation, and putts per round. Similarly, in business, it is important to identify and track key performance indicators (KPIs) that align with your goals and objectives. By focusing on relevant metrics, you can effectively measure and track your performance.

Consistency is Key

In golf, consistency is crucial for success. A player needs to have a consistent swing, approach, and mindset throughout the game. Similarly, in business, consistency in processes, strategies, and decision-making is essential for accurately measuring performance. Consistent measurement methods enable you to identify trends, track progress, and make data-driven decisions.

Course Correction

In golf, players constantly assess their performance and make adjustments to improve their game. If a shot goes off course, they make corrections to get back on track. Similarly, in business, measuring performance allows you to identify areas that need improvement or adjustments. By analyzing data and making informed decisions, you can course-correct and optimize your business operations.

Continuous Improvement

Golfers are always looking for ways to improve their skills and performance. They practice, seek feedback, and learn from their mistakes to become better players. Similarly, in business, measuring performance provides insights into areas that need improvement. It enables you to identify strengths and weaknesses, make informed decisions, and continuously improve your business processes.

Long-Term Perspective

Golf is a game that requires a long-term perspective. Players understand that one bad shot or round does not define their overall performance. Similarly, in business, it is important to have a long-term perspective when measuring performance. Focus on trends and patterns over time rather than getting discouraged by short-term fluctuations. This allows you to make strategic decisions based on the bigger picture. Overall, a game of golf teaches business owners the importance of focusing on relevant metrics, consistency, course correction, continuous improvement, and having a long-term perspective when measuring performance. By applying these lessons, business owners can effectively track their progress, identify areas for improvement, and make informed decisions to drive success.

CHAPTER 9:
MENTAL AND EMOTIONAL FACTORS AFFECTING THE GOLFER'S PERFORMANCE AND A BUSINESS OWNER'S SUCCESS

"Competitive golf is played mainly on a five-and-a-half-inch course... the space between your ears."

— Boby Jones

Both in golf and business, mental and emotional factors play a crucial role in determining an individual's performance. Successful golfers and businesspeople alike recognize the importance of mental clarity, emotional resilience, and focus in achieving their goals. Here are stories of how mental and emotional factors have impacted the performance of renowned golfers, with lessons that can be applied to the business world.

Annika Sörenstam attributes much of her success to her mental preparation and emotional resilience. Sörenstam focused not only on her physical skills but also on maintaining a positive mental attitude and managing stress effectively. She practiced mindfulness and visualization techniques to stay calm and focused during tournaments. By visualizing each shot and maintaining a clear mental picture of her desired outcomes, Sörenstam was able to perform under pressure and achieve consistent results on the course.

Annika Sörenstam's brand, ANNIKA, faced limited

growth potential primarily because of its narrow focus on golf-related products and services. By primarily concentrating on golf equipment and apparel, the brand failed to diversify its offerings and expand into other markets. One reason for this limited growth potential is the niche nature of the golf industry. While golf has a dedicated fan base and a significant market, it is still a relatively specialized sport compared to more mainstream sports like football or basketball. By solely focusing on golf-related products, ANNIKA limited its target audience to primarily golf enthusiasts, thus narrowing its potential customer base.

Furthermore, the brand's narrow focus prevented it from tapping into other revenue streams. By not venturing into areas such as lifestyle products, fitness and wellness, or collaborations with other sports and industries, ANNIKA missed out on opportunities to attract a broader range of customers who may not be avid golfers but could still be interested in the brand and its values. Additionally, the lack of diversification limited ANNIKA's ability to withstand downturns or changes in the golf industry. If there was a decline in the popularity of golf or a decrease in consumer spending on golf-related products, the brand would be heavily impacted without other revenue streams to rely on. Overall, by not diversifying its offerings and expanding beyond golf-related products, ANNIKA's brand faced limited growth potential due to its niche focus and missed opportunities to attract a broader customer base.

In business, similar techniques can be used to prepare for high-stakes meetings or presentations. Visualization and mental rehearsal can help individuals stay focused and confident, leading to better performance and outcomes.

Tiger Woods is another golfer whose mental toughness has been a key component of his success. Known for his intense focus and competitive spirit, Woods has often spoken about the importance of mental strength in his game. During the 2008 U.S. Open, Woods played through severe pain from a knee injury, demonstrating incredible mental fortitude. His ability to compartmentalize pain and stay mentally strong allowed him to win the championship, cementing his reputation as one of the greatest golfers of all time.

In the business world, leaders often face high-pressure situations that require mental resilience. Learning to stay calm and focused, even when facing significant challenges, can lead to better decision-making and ultimately, success.

Phil Mickelson, known for his strategic approach both on and off the golf course, places a strong emphasis on mental and emotional preparation. Mickelson measures his golf performance not only through traditional statistics but also by evaluating his mental clarity and emotional stability during tournaments. He practices meditation and mindfulness to maintain focus and manage stress. By staying emotionally balanced, Mickelson can make strategic decisions and perform consistently under pressure.

In business, maintaining emotional balance is equally important. Leaders who can manage their emotions effectively are better equipped to handle stress, build strong relationships, and lead their teams to success. Mental clarity and focus are essential for making sound decisions and driving performance. Entrepreneurs and business leaders often face complex challenges that require clear thinking and strategic planning. Techniques such as mindfulness, meditation, and regular breaks can help maintain mental clarity and improve focus. Emotional resilience allows individuals to bounce back from setbacks and stay motivated despite challenges. In the fast-paced business world, resilience is crucial for maintaining long-term success. Leaders who cultivate emotional resilience are better able to handle stress, navigate uncertainty, and inspire their teams.

The stories of Annika Sörenstam, Tiger Woods, and Phil Mickelson highlight the importance of mental and emotional factors in achieving peak performance. Whether on the golf course or in the boardroom, maintaining mental clarity, emotional balance, and resilience can significantly impact an individual's success. By adopting techniques such as visualization, mindfulness, and stress management, both golfers and businesspeople can enhance their performance and achieve their goals.

Here are some additional examples of professional golfers and successful entrepreneurs who are known for effectively managing their mental and emotional factors.

Brooks Koepka, an American professional golfer, has become synonymous with mental resilience and the ability to handle pressure in major championships. Known for his calm demeanor and focus, Koepka has repeatedly demonstrated how mental strength is just as crucial as physical skill in achieving success on the golf course. Brooks Koepka's journey to becoming a major champion was not without challenges. Early in his career, Koepka faced setbacks, including injuries and the struggle to establish himself on the professional circuit. However, these challenges only served to strengthen his resolve. Koepka understood that staying mentally strong was essential for overcoming obstacles and achieving his goals.

Koepka's breakthrough came at the 2017 U.S. Open at Erin Hills, where he claimed his first major championship. Throughout the tournament, Koepka maintained a laser-sharp focus, staying calm under pressure and effectively managing his emotions. His ability to stay in the moment and avoid distractions was evident as he shot a final-round sixty-seven to secure the victory. Koepka later revealed that his mental preparation, including visualization and mindfulness practices, played a significant role in his success.

Koepka's mental resilience was on display during the 2018 and 2019 PGA Championships, where he successfully defended his title. In both tournaments, Koepka faced intense competition and high-pressure situations. At the 2019 PGA Championship at Bethpage Black, he withstood a late charge from Dustin Johnson and navigated challenging course conditions to emerge victorious. Koepka's ability to manage stress and maintain a positive mindset was critical in securing back-to-back titles.

Koepka frequently speaks about the importance of staying focused and managing emotions on the golf course. In interviews, he emphasizes that maintaining a positive mindset and controlling emotions are keys to performing well under pressure. Koepka practices mental techniques such as visualization and breathing exercises to help him stay centered and calm during tournaments.

In an interview with Golf Digest, Koepka explained, "When you're out there, it's important to stay in the moment. You can't let your mind wander or think about the results. It's all about focusing on the process and taking it one shot at a time."

The mental resilience and focus that Koepka exhibits on the golf course can also be applied to the business world. Entrepreneurs and business leaders can learn from his approach by.

1. **Staying Focused:** Maintaining concentration on the task at hand and avoiding distractions can lead to better decision-making and performance.
2. **Managing Emotions:** Learning to control emotions and staying calm under pressure is essential for navigating challenging situations.
3. **Positive Mindset:** Cultivating a positive mindset and visualizing success can help individuals stay motivated and overcome obstacles.
4. **Mental Preparation:** Incorporating mental techniques such as mindfulness and visualization can enhance overall performance and resilience.

Brooks Koepka's story is a powerful testament to the importance of mental resilience and the ability to handle pressure. By staying focused, managing emotions, and maintaining a positive mindset, Koepka has achieved remarkable success in major championships. His approach offers valuable lessons not only for golfers but also for anyone aspiring to excellence in their field. Whether on the golf course or in the boardroom, mental strength and resilience are vital components of sustained success.

Elon Musk, the CEO of SpaceX and Tesla, is widely recognized for his remarkable ability to manage stress and maintain focus amidst the intense challenges of entrepreneurship. His journey is marked by relentless ambition, visionary goals, and an unwavering commitment to achieving the extraordinary. Through mindfulness practices and setting ambitious objectives, Musk has navigated numerous setbacks and driven his companies to unprecedented success.

Elon Musk's career has been punctuated by formidable obstacles. In the early days of SpaceX and Tesla, he faced financial difficulties, technical failures, and skepticism from industry experts. In 2008, both companies were on the brink of bankruptcy. SpaceX had failed in its first three launches, and Tesla struggled with production issues and financial instability.

Despite these daunting challenges, Musk's mental resilience and focus never wavered. He often cites his ability to compartmentalize stress and focus on problem-solving as critical to overcoming these early hurdles. Musk's approach to managing stress involves breaking down seemingly insurmountable problems into smaller, manageable tasks. This method, combined with his relentless work ethic, enabled him to push through the crises and lead his companies to success.

Mindfulness plays a significant role in Musk's ability to handle stress. He has spoken about the importance of mental clarity and staying present in the moment. Mindfulness techniques, such as deep breathing and meditation, help him maintain focus and make clear-headed decisions under pressure. By practicing mindfulness, Musk can keep his mind sharp and navigate the complexities of running multiple high-stakes ventures.

One of Musk's defining characteristics is his propensity for setting extraordinarily ambitious goals. Whether it's colonizing Mars, revolutionizing the automotive industry with electric vehicles, or developing sustainable energy solutions, Musk's visionary goals keep him motivated and driven. These ambitious objectives serve as a guiding star, helping him stay focused and inspired even when faced with significant setbacks.

For example, Musk's goal of making human life multiplanetary has driven SpaceX to achieve milestones once deemed impossible. The successful launch and landing of reusable rockets, the development of the Falcon Heavy, and the ongoing progress of the Starship project all stem from Musk's unwavering commitment to his ambitious vision.

Musk's journey has not been without its share of setbacks. From production delays at Tesla to launch failures at SpaceX, he has faced numerous challenges that could have derailed his plans. However, Musk's ability to maintain focus and resilience has been crucial in overcoming these obstacles. He views setbacks as opportunities for learning and growth, constantly iterating and improving his approach.

In a 2018 interview with *60 Minutes,* Musk discussed the immense pressure he faced during Tesla's Model 3 production ramp-up. He revealed that he was working up to 120 hours a week, sleeping on the factory floor to ensure that production goals were met. Despite the physical and mental toll, Musk's determination and focus on the end goal enabled Tesla to overcome its "production hell" and achieve record deliveries.

Elon Musk's story is a powerful testament to the importance of managing stress, maintaining focus, and setting ambitious goals. His practices of mindfulness, problem-solving, and relentless perseverance have enabled him to navigate through significant challenges and achieve extraordinary success. Musk's approach provides valuable lessons for entrepreneurs and leaders, demonstrating that mental resilience and a clear vision are essential components of sustained success. Whether through mindfulness techniques or the pursuit of visionary goals, Musk's methods offer a blueprint for achieving greatness in the face of adversity.

Oprah Winfrey, a media mogul and philanthropist, has built an empire through her unparalleled work ethic, resilience, and dedication to personal growth. Throughout her illustrious career, Oprah has openly discussed the importance of meditation and mindfulness in managing stress and maintaining emotional well-being. She believes that self-reflection and self-care are crucial for both personal and professional growth, principles that have guided her journey to success.

Oprah's path to success was not easy. Born into poverty in rural Mississippi, she faced numerous challenges growing up, including a tumultuous family life and various forms of abuse. Despite these hardships, Oprah's determination and talent shone through. She began her career in the media as a news anchor, eventually finding her true calling as a talk show host with "The Oprah Winfrey Show."

As her career soared, so did the pressures and demands of her professional life. Managing a daily talk show, running a production company, and overseeing various business ventures took a toll on her mental and emotional health. It was during these high-pressure years that Oprah discovered the transformative power of meditation and mindfulness.

Oprah's journey into meditation began in the early 1990s when she invited Deepak Chopra, a renowned spiritual leader, onto her show. This encounter sparked her interest in mindfulness practices. Over the years, Oprah has integrated meditation into her daily routine, finding it to be a powerful tool for managing stress and maintaining emotional well-being. In numerous interviews, Oprah has shared how meditation helps her stay grounded and focused. She often starts her day with a period of quiet reflection, using techniques such as deep breathing and guided visualization to center herself. This practice not only helps her manage the stresses of her demanding career but also enhances her clarity and decision-making abilities.

Oprah believes deeply in the power of self-reflection for

personal and professional growth. She regularly engages in introspective practices, such as journaling and spending time in nature, to gain insight into her thoughts and emotions. This self-awareness allows her to address personal challenges proactively and maintain a balanced life.

In her book "What I Know For Sure," Oprah writes about the importance of tuning into oneself to understand one's true desires and motivations. She emphasizes that self-reflection has been instrumental in her journey, helping her to align her actions with her values and purpose.

Oprah's commitment to self-care extends beyond meditation and mindfulness. She is a strong advocate for maintaining a healthy lifestyle, which includes regular exercise, a balanced diet, and adequate sleep. Oprah often speaks about the significance of taking care of one's body to support mental and emotional health.

In addition to physical self-care, Oprah places a high value on nurturing her emotional well-being. She surrounds herself with positive influences, maintains strong personal relationships, and engages in activities that bring her joy and fulfillment. This holistic approach to self-care has enabled her to sustain her energy and passion throughout her career.

Oprah Winfrey's story is a testament to the transformative power of meditation, mindfulness, and self-care. By embracing these practices, she has been able to manage stress, maintain emotional well-being, and achieve remarkable success. Oprah's journey highlights the importance of self-reflection and self-care for personal and professional growth, offering valuable lessons for anyone striving to lead a balanced and fulfilling life.

Oprah often shares her experiences and insights with her audience, inspiring millions to explore mindfulness and prioritize their well-being. Her story serves as a powerful reminder that true success is not just about professional achievements but also about cultivating a healthy and balanced life.

Sara Blakely, the founder of Spanx, has highlighted the

role of positive thinking and visualization in her entrepreneurial journey. She credits these practices for helping her overcome self-doubt and stay focused on her goals. In the late 1990s, Sara Blakely was working as a fax machine saleswoman in Florida. Frustrated with the look of pantyhose under white pants, she had an idea to create a new type of undergarment that would be both comfortable and flattering. Despite having no background in fashion design or business, Blakely was determined to turn her idea into a reality.

From the start, Blakely faced numerous challenges. She had to learn about manufacturing, patenting, and marketing from scratch. Moreover, many people, including potential investors, were skeptical of her idea. However, Blakely credits her practice of positive thinking and visualization for helping her push through these doubts and setbacks.

Blakely often speaks about how she visualized her success long before it became a reality. She imagined her product on store shelves and pictured herself as a successful entrepreneur. This mental imagery helped her stay motivated and focused, even when the odds seemed stacked against her. She believed that if she could see it in her mind, she could make it happen.

Blakely's use of visualization was not just about imagining the end goal; she also visualized overcoming obstacles along the way. For instance, when she faced rejections from manufacturers, she visualized finding the right partner who would believe in her vision. This positive mindset kept her resilient and persistent.

In interviews, Blakely has shared how she used visualization to prepare for important meetings and presentations. By mentally rehearsing these scenarios, she was able to approach them with confidence and clarity. This practice was crucial when she finally secured a meeting with Neiman Marcus, which led to Spanx being stocked in their stores.

Blakely's unwavering belief in her vision paid off. Spanx quickly became a sensation, revolutionizing the shapewear industry. Her success story is often highlighted as an example of how positive thinking and visualization can transform a seemingly impossible dream into a reality.

Spanx's success brought Blakely immense financial rewards, but she remained grounded and committed to her principles. She used her platform to inspire other entrepreneurs, emphasizing the importance of maintaining a positive mindset and visualizing success. Blakely also became a philanthropist, focusing on empowering women and supporting entrepreneurial ventures.

Sara Blakely's journey offers valuable lessons for aspiring entrepreneurs.

1. **Positive Thinking:** Maintaining a positive outlook can help overcome self-doubt and keep you motivated.

2. **Visualization:** Visualizing your goals and the steps to achieve them can create a mental road map to success.

3. **Persistence:** Believing in your vision and staying resilient in the face of setbacks is crucial.

4. **Self-Belief:** Confidence in your ideas and capabilities can drive you to push boundaries and achieve extraordinary results. Sara Blakely's story is a powerful reminder of the impact positive thinking and visualization can have on an entrepreneurial journey. By believing in her vision and using mental practices to stay focused and motivated, Blakely turned a simple idea into a billion-dollar business. Her success continues to inspire countless individuals to harness the power of their minds to achieve their dreams.

Richard Branson has emphasized the importance of resilience and adaptability in entrepreneurship. He employs stress-management techniques such as exercise, kiteboarding, and spending time with loved ones to maintain a healthy work-life balance. Here are a few examples.

1. **Exercise:** Branson believes in the power of physical activity to reduce stress and improve well-being. He engages in various forms of exercise, including kiteboarding, tennis, and cycling, to stay active and energized.

2. **Spending Time with Loved Ones**: Branson prioritizes spending quality time with his family and loved ones. He recognizes the importance of nurturing personal relationships and finds joy in their company, which helps him recharge and find balance.

3. **Pursuing Hobbies and Interests:** Branson enjoys pursuing hobbies and interests outside of work. He engages in activities like playing the guitar, writing, and exploring nature. These hobbies provide him with a sense of fulfillment and relaxation.

4. **Taking Breaks and Vacations:** Branson understands the value of taking breaks and unplugging from work. He regularly takes vacations to recharge and rejuvenate. This helps him maintain perspective, reduce stress, and come back to work with renewed focus and creativity.

5. **Delegating and Empowering Others:** Branson believes in delegating responsibilities and empowering his team. By trusting his team members and giving them autonomy, he reduces his workload and stress levels, allowing him to maintain a healthier work-life balance.

These techniques, among others, have helped Richard Branson manage stress and maintain a healthy work-life balance throughout his entrepreneurial journey.

Richard Branson prioritizes spending quality time with his family and loved ones for several reasons.

Emotional well-being: Spending time with loved ones allows Branson to nurture his personal relationships and strengthen the emotional bonds he shares with his family.

This connection provides him with a sense of love, support, and belonging, which contributes to his overall emotional well-being.

By dedicating time to his family, Branson is able to achieve a balance between his personal and professional life. This helps him maintain perspective and prevents him from becoming solely consumed by work-related stress and responsibilities.

Branson recognizes that life is not solely about work and business success. By prioritizing time with his family, he can enjoy the rewards of his hard work and experience the joys and fulfillment that come from personal relationships.

Spending time with loved ones can inspire and motivate Branson. It allows him to see the impact of his success on his family and loved ones, giving him a sense of purpose and drive to continue his entrepreneurial endeavors.

Research has shown that strong social connections and relationships are linked to better mental and physical health. By prioritizing time with his family, Branson is investing in his well-being and reducing the negative effects of stress.

Overall, Richard Branson prioritizes spending quality time with his family and loved ones because it brings him happiness, balance, perspective, and a sense of fulfillment, all of which contribute to his overall well-being and success.

These individuals serve as inspiring examples of how managing mental and emotional factors can contribute to success in both golf and entrepreneurship.

When it comes to business success, my Harvard Business School classmate Peter invests in medium-sized businesses in Germany. His ability to make sound decisions is crucial for his success. Mental factors such as clarity of thought, critical thinking skills, and emotional intelligence play a significant role in effective decision-making. Peter's leadership skills are vital for his success, and effective leadership requires mental and emotional intelligence to inspire and motivate his employees, handle conflicts, and make tough decisions. Emotional factors such as empathy, self-awareness, and the ability to manage stress can greatly impact a business owner's leadership effectiveness.

The business landscape is constantly evolving, and success often hinges on adaptability. Peter's mental factors, like open-mindedness, flexibility, and the ability to embrace change, are critical for his success. Emotional factors such as resilience and the ability to manage uncertainty help him navigate challenges and seize new opportunities. Effective communication is essential for building relationships, managing teams, and attracting customers. Peter's clarity of thought, active listening, and the ability to articulate ideas play a significant role in successful communication. Emotional factors such as empathy, emotional awareness, and the ability to manage emotions also enhance his communication effectiveness.

Running his business is stressful, and his ability to manage stress is crucial for his success. Mental and emotional factors such as self-care, stress coping mechanisms, and work-life balance impact his overall well-being and ability to perform at his best.

These examples highlight the significant influence of mental and emotional factors on a golfer's performance and a business owner's success. Developing and nurturing these factors can greatly enhance performance and outcomes in both domains. Some mental and emotional factors that can affect both a golfer's performance and a business owner's success include.

Confidence and Self-Belief

Confidence plays a vital role in both golf and business. Golfers who lack confidence in their abilities may second-guess their shots, leading to inconsistency and poor performance. Similarly, business owners who lack confidence in their decisions or the potential of their business may struggle to take risks and seize opportunities for growth and success.

Focus and Concentration

Both golf and business require a high level of focus and concentration. Golfers who struggle to maintain focus during a round may find it challenging to execute shots accurately or make effective decisions. Similarly, business owners who struggle to stay focused on their goals and priorities may lose sight of important tasks and opportunities, hindering their chances of success.

Resilience and Perseverance

Both golf and business involve setbacks and failures. Golfers who are not resilient and struggle to bounce back from bad shots or poor rounds may become demoralized and see a decline in performance. Similarly, business owners who are not resilient in the face of challenges and setbacks may give up too easily or struggle to adapt and find alternative solutions, affecting their chances of success.

Emotional Management

Emotions can significantly impact performance and decision-making. Golfers who struggle to manage their emotions, such as frustration, anger, or nervousness, may make impulsive and poor decisions on the course. Similarly, business owners who have difficulty managing their emotions during stressful situations or when faced with setbacks may make hasty decisions that can negatively impact their business.

Goal Setting and Motivation

Both golf and business require clear goals and motivation. Golfers who lack clear goals or motivation may struggle to maintain focus and drive during practice and competitions. Similarly, business owners who do not set specific and achievable goals or lack motivation may find it challenging to stay committed and take the necessary actions to achieve success.

Positive Mindset and Self-Talk

A positive mindset and self-talk are crucial in both golf and business. Golfers who engage in negative self-talk or have a pessimistic outlook may undermine their confidence and performance. Similarly, business owners who have a negative mindset or constantly doubt their abilities may limit their potential for success.

Stress and Pressure Management

Both golf and business can involve high levels of stress and pressure. Golfers who struggle to manage stress and perform under pressure may experience a decline in performance during important tournaments or critical moments. Similarly, business owners who are unable to manage stress and pressure may struggle to make sound decisions or effectively lead their teams during challenging times.

It's important for both golfers and business owners to recognize and address these mental and emotional factors. Techniques such as visualization, mindfulness, goal setting, seeking support from coaches or mentors, and practicing emotional regulation can help improve mental and emotional well-being, leading to better performance in golf and increased success in business.

CHAPTER 10:
WHAT QUALITIES ARE
IMPORTANT FOR SUCCESS?

"Moral authority comes from following universal and timeless principles like honesty, integrity, treating people with respect."
— Stephen Covey

Success in both business and golf requires a unique blend of qualities that enable individuals to overcome challenges, stay focused on their goals, and achieve excellence. Qualities such as mental resilience, strategic thinking, focus and concentration, adaptability, and a positive mindset are crucial for achieving success in both business and golf. By cultivating these qualities, individuals can navigate challenges, stay focused on their goals, and achieve excellence in their respective fields. Take, for example, Elon Musk and Tiger Woods.

Tiger Woods is known for his unwavering dedication to his craft. He has spent countless hours practicing and honing his skills, even in the face of adversity and setbacks. This relentless pursuit of excellence has contributed to his success in the world of golf. Tiger Woods possesses exceptional mental strength, allowing him to stay focused and composed under pressure. He has demonstrated the ability to maintain his composure during high-stakes tournaments, making crucial shots when it matters most.

Elon Musk is renowned for his visionary mindset. He can imagine and conceptualize groundbreaking ideas that push the boundaries of technology and innovation. This visionary thinking has led to the creation of companies like SpaceX and Tesla, revolutionizing industries. Elon Musk is not afraid to take risks and pursue ambitious endeavors. He embraces challenges and tackles them head-on, even when faced with skepticism or obstacles. This fearlessness has allowed him to disrupt traditional industries and achieve remarkable success.

These qualities, whether in the world of professional golf or entrepreneurship, play a significant role in the achievements of individuals like Tiger Woods and Elon Musk. Dedication and perseverance are crucial qualities that contribute to the success of professionals like Tiger Woods and Elon Musk in the following ways.

Mastery of Skills

Dedication and perseverance drive these individuals to consistently work hard and improve their skills. Tiger Woods' dedication to practice and continuous improvement has helped him master the intricacies of golf, allowing him to excel on the course. Similarly, Elon Musk's commitment to learning and pushing boundaries has enabled him to become an expert in various fields, from aerospace engineering to electric vehicles.

Overcoming Challenges

Both Tiger Woods and Elon Musk have faced numerous challenges throughout their careers. Dedication and perseverance give them the resilience to overcome setbacks and obstacles. They view challenges as opportunities for growth rather than reasons to give up. This mindset allows them to stay focused, adapt their strategies, and find innovative solutions to problems.

Goal Achievement

Dedication and perseverance help professionals set and achieve ambitious goals. Tiger Woods and Elon Musk have set high standards for themselves and continuously strive to surpass them. Their unwavering commitment to their goals keeps them motivated and focused, even in the face of adversity or setbacks.

Long-Term Success

Success in any field requires consistent effort and a long-term perspective. Dedication and perseverance enable professionals to stay committed to their vision and work toward it over an extended period. Tiger Woods and Elon Musk have both demonstrated the ability to sustain their success by staying dedicated to their craft and maintaining a long-term view of their goals.

Additional qualities to achieve success include the following.

Integrity

Warren Buffett places a high value on integrity. He believes that integrity is the most important quality to look for in people when building a successful organization. Buffett emphasizes the importance of surrounding oneself with individuals who possess integrity, honesty, and ethical behavior. Building a culture of integrity helps foster trust and credibility, both internally within the organization and externally with customers and stakeholders.

Competence and Expertise

Buffett emphasizes the importance of competence and expertise in the people you hire and work with. He believes that surrounding yourself with individuals who are highly skilled and knowledgeable in their respective fields is crucial for long-term success. Buffett looks for individuals who have a deep understanding of the industry and possess the necessary expertise to make informed decisions.

Strong Work Ethic

Buffett believes in the power of hard work and a strong work ethic. He values individuals who are dedicated, committed, and willing to put in the effort required to achieve success. Buffett himself is known for his disciplined work routine and long-term commitment to his investments. He encourages individuals to have a strong work ethic and to be willing to go the extra mile to achieve their goals.

Rationality and Sound Judgment

Buffett emphasizes the importance of rationality and sound judgment in decision-making. He looks for individuals who can think critically, analyze data, and make informed decisions based on logic and reason. Buffett believes that avoiding impulsive and emotional decision-making is crucial for long-term success in business.

Long-Term Perspective

Buffett is known for his long-term perspective when it comes to investing and building businesses. He believes in making decisions that have a long-term impact rather than focusing on short-term gains. Buffett is looking for individuals who share this long-term mindset and are willing to invest time and effort into building sustainable and successful organizations.

Warren Buffett believes that qualities such as integrity, competence, strong work ethic, rationality, and a long-term perspective are important when building a successful organization. By prioritizing these qualities, entrepreneurs and business leaders can lay a strong foundation for their organizations and increase their chances of long-term success.

Tiger Woods has also highlighted several important qualities that are crucial for playing a successful game of golf. Here are some of the qualities he emphasizes.

Skill and Technique

Woods believes that developing and honing golfing skills and techniques are fundamental to success in the game. This includes mastering the fundamentals of the swing, grip, posture, and alignment. Woods himself is known for his exceptional technical skills and dedication to continuously improving his game. He emphasizes the importance of practicing and refining one's skills to achieve consistent performance on the course.

Mental Toughness and Focus

Woods recognizes the significance of mental toughness and focus in golf. He believes that maintaining a strong and focused mindset, even in challenging situations, is essential for success. Woods emphasizes the importance of staying calm, managing emotions, and making clear decisions under pressure. Building mental resilience and staying focused throughout the game are key qualities he highlights.

Physical Fitness and Endurance

Woods emphasizes the importance of physical fitness and endurance in golf. He believes that being physically fit enables golfers to maintain consistency in their swing and perform at their best for the duration of a game. Woods is known for his rigorous fitness regimen and highlights the correlation between physical well-being and optimal golf performance.

Strategic Thinking and Course Management

Woods stresses the significance of strategic thinking and course management in golf. He advises golfers to carefully analyze the course, assess risks, and make smart decisions about shot selection and club choice. Woods emphasizes the importance of understanding one's strengths and weaknesses and adapting the game plan accordingly to maximize performance.

Perseverance and Resilience

Woods recognizes the importance of perseverance and resilience in golf. He believes that setbacks and failures are part of the game and that it is essential to bounce back and learn from them. Woods himself has faced numerous challenges and setbacks throughout his career but has demonstrated resilience and the ability to come back stronger.

Tiger Woods places significant emphasis on the importance of mental toughness and focus in golf. He believes that these qualities are crucial for success in the game and can make a significant difference in a golfer's performance. Here's how Woods views the importance of mental toughness and focus in golf.

Managing Pressure

Woods understands that golf is a mentally challenging sport, especially when playing in high-pressure situations. He believes that mental toughness is essential for managing pressure effectively. Woods emphasizes the importance of staying calm, composed, and focused, even when facing intense competition or difficult shots. He believes that mental resilience is key to performing well under pressure and making sound decisions.

Concentration and Focus

Woods stresses the significance of concentration and focus during a golf game. He believes that maintaining a high level of focus throughout the round is crucial for consistent performance. Woods emphasizes the need to block out distractions, stay fully present in the moment, and focus on each shot individually. He believes that a momentary lapse in concentration can have a significant impact on the outcome of a game.

Overcoming Adversity

Woods acknowledges that golf is a sport that presents numerous challenges and obstacles. He believes that mental toughness is necessary for overcoming adversity and bouncing back from setbacks. Woods himself has faced several personal and professional challenges throughout his career and has demonstrated resilience and the ability to come back stronger. He encourages golfers to develop a resilient mindset and view setbacks as opportunities for growth.

Visualizing Success

Woods advocates for the power of visualization in golf. He believes that mentally visualizing successful shots and outcomes can positively impact performance. Woods emphasizes the importance of creating a clear mental image of the desired result before executing a shot. He believes that visualization helps golfers focus their minds and increase the chances of achieving the desired outcome.

Managing Emotions

Woods understands the importance of managing emotions on the golf course. He believes that emotional control is essential for making rational decisions and maintaining a steady performance. Woods encourages golfers to stay composed, avoid getting too high or too low emotionally, and channel their energy into productive actions.

Tiger Woods views mental toughness and focus as vital components of success in golf. He believes that managing pressure, maintaining concentration, overcoming adversity, visualizing success, and managing emotions are all key aspects of developing mental toughness. By cultivating these qualities, golfers can enhance their performance and achieve success on the golf course.

Tiger Woods emphasizes the importance of skill and technique, mental toughness and focus, physical fitness and endurance, strategic thinking, and course management, as well as perseverance and resilience when playing a successful golf game. By embodying these qualities, golfers can enhance their performance on the course and increase their chances of achieving success in the game.

Elon Musk possesses several key qualities that have contributed to his ability to create and build successful companies.

Visionary Leadership

Musk has a clear and ambitious vision for the future. He is known for his ability to think big and set audacious goals. His vision inspires and motivates his teams to work toward a common purpose, driving innovation and pushing boundaries.

Perseverance and Resilience: Musk has demonstrated remarkable perseverance in the face of challenges and setbacks. He has experienced numerous obstacles and failures throughout his career, but he has consistently shown resilience, bouncing back and learning from each experience. His determination to overcome obstacles has been crucial in achieving his goals.

Risk-Taking and Boldness

Musk is not afraid to take risks and pursue unconventional ideas. He is willing to challenge the status quo and disrupt industries. His willingness to take bold steps, such as starting SpaceX and Tesla, has set him apart from traditional approaches and has been instrumental in his success.

Deep Technical Knowledge

Musk possesses a strong technical background and a deep understanding of the industries he operates in. His expertise in engineering and physics allows him to make informed decisions and drive innovation within his companies. This technical knowledge enables him to identify opportunities and solve complex problems.

Ability to Attract and Lead Talented Teams

Musk has a unique ability to attract top talent and build teams of exceptional individuals. He fosters a culture of innovation, encourages creativity, and empowers his teams to take ownership and make meaningful contributions. His leadership style emphasizes collaboration and encourages a sense of purpose among his employees.

Long-Term Thinking

Musk is known for his long-term perspective and commitment to making a lasting impact. He is not solely focused on short-term gains but rather on building sustainable businesses that can drive significant change and improve the world. This long-term thinking allows him to make strategic decisions that align with his broader vision.

Elon Musk's qualities of visionary leadership, perseverance, risk-taking, technical expertise, ability to attract talent, and long-term thinking have been instrumental in his ability to create and build successful companies. These qualities have enabled him to disrupt industries, drive innovation, and make a significant impact in areas such as space exploration, electric vehicles, and renewable energy.

As an immigrant from Ecuador, my journey to success in the United States has been marked by a combination of essential qualities that have helped me overcome challenges, seize opportunities, and build a thriving career. Each of the following qualities played a pivotal role in my story, shaping my path and enabling me to achieve my goals.

Mental resilience has been my anchor throughout this journey. Leaving behind the familiar surroundings of Ecuador and starting anew in a foreign country was daunting. There were moments of doubt and setbacks that tested my resolve. However, I learned to navigate these challenges with determination and a positive outlook.

Strategic thinking and setting clear goals have been critical in charting my path. When I first arrived in the U.S., I understood the importance of identifying market trends and making informed decisions. I set clear, achievable goals for my education and career. I focused on understanding my career opportunities and positioning myself for success. This strategic approach helped me anticipate opportunities and challenges, allowing me to make decisions that aligned with my long-term vision.

Managing multiple tasks and making sound decisions required immense focus and concentration. Balancing work, studies, and personal life was not easy, but staying focused on my priorities helped me stay on track. By dedicating time to each task and minimizing distractions, I was able to achieve high performance in most areas of my life.) Adaptability has been essential for responding to market changes and staying competitive. The dynamic nature of the business world demands flexibility and the ability to pivot when necessary. Whether it was learning new skills, embracing technology, or adjusting to new roles, my willingness to adapt ensured that I remained relevant and competitive in my field.

A positive mindset has been the cornerstone of my success, fostering creativity, resilience, and a can-do attitude. Embracing positivity allowed me to view challenges as opportunities for growth and innovation. This mindset was inspired by the teachings of motivational figures like Tony Robbins, who advocates for the power of positive thinking and its impact on achieving success. By maintaining an optimistic outlook, I was able to stay motivated, overcome obstacles, and continuously strive for excellence.

My journey from Ecuador to achieving success in the United States is a testament to the power of mental resilience, strategic thinking, focus, adaptability, and a positive mindset. Each of these qualities has been instrumental in navigating challenges, seizing opportunities, and achieving my goals. By embodying these principles, I have been able to create a fulfilling and successful life in a new country, proving that with the right mindset and strategies, anything is possible. These qualities will also help you in your pursuit of excellence and enable you to make significant contributions in your respective fields.

Success, whether on the golf course or in the business world, is often a journey marked by determination, clear goals, and a passion for what you do. My recent experience at the LPGA West Palm Beach Chapter's Pink Ball fundraising event perfectly encapsulates this journey. It was an event that brought together my love for golf, my thriving real estate business, and my philanthropic endeavors.

Recently, on a beautiful sunny morning, I found myself at the Little Club in Delray Beach, FL playing golf with friends and colleagues. We were enjoying our annual Pink Ball event; it was more than just a game – it was a celebration and a fundraiser to support younger golfers aspiring to achieve their dreams. As we teed off, the camaraderie and friendly competition filled the air with electric energy, enthusiasm, and high expectations.

The day was meticulously planned, featuring not only the golf tournament but also a delightful fashion show where I had the pleasure of modeling ladies' golf attire. The fusion of style and sport was a testament to the multifaceted nature of our passions and how they can be harmoniously intertwined. We enjoyed a sumptuous lunch, engaged in lively conversations, and celebrated each other's achievements with numerous prizes. This event was also a great opportunity for me to promote my real estate business. Golf has always been a powerful networking tool, and this day was no different. Engaging with fellow golfers, sharing market insights, and showcasing my latest listings seamlessly integrated business with pleasure. The genuine connections made on the golf course often lead to lasting professional relationships and successful deals.

Reflecting on this day, I realize the importance of having clear goals and expectations. Golf, much like business, requires focus, strategy, and a positive mindset. These principles have guided me throughout my career, helping me navigate challenges and celebrate successes.

Looking back, I see a life filled with purpose and joy, surrounded by supportive friends and colleagues. The combination of playing golf, promoting my business, and enjoying the finer aspects of life like fashion and good company brings a sense of fulfillment that is truly priceless. It's a reminder that success is not just about financial gains, but about living a balanced, joyful life where your passions fuel your achievements.

This book is not only the culmination of my experiences but also a testament to the power of combining passion with professionalism. It proves that with clear goals and a positive outlook, one can achieve success both on the golf course and in the business world. My fervent desire for you is that this book will help you in your pursuit of excellence and enable you to make significant contributions in your respective fields.

CHAPTER 11:
WHY GOLF PLAYERS AND BUSINESS OWNERS FAIL?

*"Whether you think you can,
or you think you can't – you're right."*

– Henry Ford

There can be various reasons why some golfers may struggle and be considered "bad" players, just as there are reasons why some business owners may fail.

Failure is a common experience for both golf players and business owners. The reasons for these failures often overlap, involving factors such as lack of mental resilience, poor strategic planning, insufficient focus, resistance to adaptability, and a negative mindset. Let me share a personal story to illustrate these points and explain how individuals can overcome these obstacles to achieve success.

Several years ago, I embarked on a journey to establish my consulting business while simultaneously pursuing my passion for golf. Both endeavors were fraught with challenges and moments of doubt. Initially, my consulting business struggled to gain traction, and my performance on the golf course was inconsistent. It became evident that the reasons for these struggles were interconnected.

Lack of Mental Resilience

In golf, mental resilience is critical. Players often face high-pressure situations that can lead to mistakes and frustration. Without the mental toughness to recover, these mistakes can compound, leading to poor performance. Similarly, business owners face constant challenges, from market fluctuations to competition. A lack of mental resilience can result in giving up too soon or making poor decisions under stress. To build mental resilience, both golfers and business owners should practice mindfulness and stress management techniques. Regular meditation, deep breathing exercises, and setting aside time for self-reflection can help maintain a positive outlook and recover quickly from setbacks. In my journey, incorporating mindfulness practices allowed me to stay calm under pressure and approach challenges with a clear mind.

Poor Strategic Planning

Without a strategic approach, golfers may fail to navigate the course effectively, leading to inconsistent results. Each shot requires planning and consideration of various factors such as wind, terrain, and hazards. In business, poor strategic planning can result in misaligned goals, wasted resources, and missed opportunities. Without a clear strategy, businesses may struggle to adapt to changing market conditions or achieve long-term growth.

To improve strategic planning, both golfers and business owners should set clear, achievable goals and develop detailed plans to reach them. This involves regular analysis and adjustments based on performance metrics. For my consulting business, creating a detailed business plan with specific milestones helped me stay focused and measure progress effectively.

Insufficient Focus

Focus is essential in golf to ensure precision and consistency. Distractions or a wandering mind can lead to missed shots and poor performance. In business, multitasking and lack of focus can result in errors, missed deadlines, and reduced productivity. It's crucial to prioritize tasks and maintain concentration on key objectives.

Improving focus requires discipline and structured routines. Techniques such as time-blocking, where specific periods are dedicated to tasks, can enhance concentration. In my experience, setting aside uninterrupted time for both business planning and golf practice allowed me to achieve better results in both areas.

Resistance to Adaptability

The ability to adapt to changing conditions, such as weather or course layout, is vital for golfers. Rigidly sticking to one approach can lead to failure when circumstances change. Businesses must adapt to evolving market trends, customer needs, and technological advancements. Resistance to change can result in stagnation and decline.

Embracing adaptability involves staying informed about trends and being willing to pivot when necessary. For my consulting business, regularly updating my knowledge and being open to new strategies helped me stay competitive. On the golf course, learning to adjust my techniques based on conditions improved my game significantly.

Negative Mindset

A negative mindset can lead to self-doubt and decreased performance in golf. Confidence is key to executing successful shots. In business, a negative mindset can stifle creativity and innovation. It can also impact team morale and productivity.

Cultivating a positive mindset involves focusing on strengths, celebrating small successes, and maintaining a growth-oriented perspective. For me, adopting a positive mindset meant viewing challenges as opportunities for growth, which not only boosted my confidence but also inspired my team.

Turning Setbacks into Stepping Stones: Lessons from Failure

Greg Norman experienced failure with his company Great White Shark Enterprises. Despite being advised to diversify his business interests, he focused heavily on golf-related ventures and investments. This lack of diversification left him vulnerable to market fluctuations, and when the golf industry faced a downturn, his business suffered. Norman's failure to heed advice and diversify his business portfolio contributed to his setback.

Annika Sörenstam faced failure with her ANNIKA brand. Despite being advised to expand her brand beyond golf-related products and services, she primarily focused on golf equipment and apparel. This limited scope hindered her brand's growth potential and limited its appeal to a broader customer base. Sörenstam's failure to diversify her brand and explore new markets led to a lack of sustainable growth. Arnold Palmer experienced failure with his company Arnold Palmer Enterprises. Despite being advised to adapt to changing consumer preferences and invest in digital marketing and e-commerce, he remained heavily reliant on traditional marketing methods and brick-and-mortar retail. This failure to embrace digital transformation and evolve with the times resulted in a decline in his business's competitiveness and profitability.

Michelle Wie, a professional golfer and business owner, faced failure with her clothing line, MWear. Despite being advised to conduct thorough market research and develop a strong brand identity, she rushed into launching her clothing line without fully understanding her target market's preferences and needs. This lack of market understanding led to poor sales and limited customer appeal. Wie's failure to invest time in market research and brand development contributed to the setback of her clothing line.

In each of these cases, the golfers-turned-business owners faced failure due to various factors such as lack of diversification, failure to adapt to changing market trends, reliance on traditional methods, and inadequate market research. Despite being advised, they either did not take the advice seriously or overlooked the importance of certain business strategies, leading to their respective setbacks.

There can be various reasons for the struggle. Here are some common factors that can contribute to these outcomes.

Lack of Skill Development

Golf requires a combination of technical skills, such as proper swing mechanics, putting technique, and course management. If golfers do not invest sufficient time and effort in developing and honing these skills, their performance may suffer. Similarly, business owners need to acquire and continuously improve the skills necessary to run a successful business, such as financial management, marketing, and leadership. Without adequate skill development, both golfers and business owners may struggle to achieve their desired outcomes.

Inconsistent Practice and Preparation

Consistent practice and preparation are crucial for success in both golf and business. Golfers who do not dedicate enough time to practice and fail to prepare adequately for each round may struggle to perform at their best. Similarly, business owners who do not invest sufficient time in strategic planning, market research, and staying updated on industry trends may find it challenging to navigate the competitive business landscape.

Mental and Emotional Factors

Golf and business both involve mental and emotional aspects that can impact performance and success. Golfers who struggle with mental toughness, focus, and managing pressure may find it difficult to perform consistently. Similarly, business owners who are unable to handle stress, make tough decisions, or bounce back from failures may face challenges in their entrepreneurial journey.

Lack of Adaptability and Resilience

Golf and business environments are dynamic and require adaptability and resilience. Golfers who are resistant to change struggle to adjust to different course conditions or learn from mistakes, making it difficult to improve their performance. Likewise, business owners who resist adapting to market changes, customer preferences, or emerging technologies may struggle to stay relevant and competitive.

External Factors and Circumstances

It's important to acknowledge that external factors and circumstances can also influence performance and success. In golf, weather conditions, course difficulty, and competition level can impact a golfer's performance. Similarly, in business, economic conditions, market saturation, and unexpected challenges can affect a business owner's ability to succeed.

It's worth noting that success in golf and business is a complex interplay of various factors, and individual circumstances can differ. Some golfers may struggle due to technical or mental limitations, while others may face external challenges beyond their control. Similarly, business owners may fail due to a combination of internal and external factors. Continuous learning, adaptability, resilience, and a willingness to seek support and guidance can help both golfers and business owners improve their performance and increase their chances of success.

There are common factors that contribute to both a golfer's poor performance and a business owner's failure to achieve revenues and profitability.

Lack of Skill Development and Knowledge

Both golf and business require a certain level of skill and knowledge for success. In golf, if a player does not invest time and effort into developing technical skills, such as swing mechanics or putting technique, their performance may suffer. Similarly, business owners need to acquire and continuously improve their skills in areas like marketing, finance, and operations. Without adequate skill development and knowledge, both golfers and business owners may struggle to achieve their desired outcomes.

Inconsistent Practice and Preparation

Consistent practice and preparation are crucial for success in both golf and business. Golfers who do not dedicate enough time to practice and fail to adequately prepare for each round may struggle to perform at their best. Similarly, business owners who do not invest sufficient time in strategic planning, market research, and staying updated on industry trends may find it challenging to generate revenues and profitability.

Mental and Emotional Factors

Both golf and business involve mental and emotional aspects that can impact performance and success. Golfers who struggle with mental toughness, focus, and managing pressure may find it difficult to perform consistently. Similarly, business owners who are unable to handle stress, make tough decisions, or bounce back from failures may face challenges in achieving revenues and profitability.

Lack of Adaptability and Resilience

Both golf and business environments are dynamic and require adaptability and resilience. Golfers who are resistant to change, struggle to adjust to different course conditions or are unable to learn from their mistakes may find it difficult to improve their performance. Likewise, business owners who are unwilling to adapt to market changes, customer preferences, or emerging technologies may struggle to generate revenues and achieve profitability.

External Factors and Circumstances

It's important to acknowledge that external factors and circumstances can also influence performance and success in both golf and business. In golf, factors such as weather conditions, course difficulty, and competition level can impact a golfer's performance. Similarly, in business, factors such as economic conditions, market saturation, and unexpected challenges can affect a business owner's ability to generate revenues and achieve profitability.

Financial Management

Both golfers and business owners need to have a solid understanding of financial management. Golfers who do not manage their golf-related expenses effectively, such as equipment costs, membership fees, and travel expenses, may struggle to sustain their performance. Similarly, business owners who do not effectively manage their finances, including budgeting, cash flow, and expenses, may face challenges in achieving revenues and profitability.

Marketing and Customer Engagement

For both golfers and business owners, effective marketing and customer engagement are essential. Golfers who do not effectively market themselves, build relationships with sponsors, or engage with fans may struggle to attract opportunities for sponsorships or endorsements. Similarly, business owners who do not effectively market their products or services, build relationships with customers, or engage with their target audience may struggle to generate revenues and achieve profitability.

Failure is a natural part of the journey for both golf players and business owners. By understanding and addressing the common reasons for failure – such as lack of mental resilience, poor strategic planning, insufficient focus, resistance to adaptability, and a negative mindset – individuals can overcome these obstacles and achieve success. My experience has shown that with the right strategies and mindset, it is possible to navigate challenges and reach one's goals.

For those seeking to enhance their performance in business, my consulting services offer personalized guidance and support to help you build resilience, develop effective strategies, and maintain a positive outlook. By working together, we can turn obstacles into stepping stones toward success.

CHAPTER 12:
THE PGA TOUR'S PARALLEL LESSONS BETWEEN GOLF AND BUSINESS

*"Success in golf depends less on strength of body
and more on strength of mind and character."*

– Arnold Palmer

This is a bonus chapter about the PGA Tour. I want to share some more of the parallels between golf and business that can be beneficial because the PGA Tour is widely recognized as the premier professional golf tour in the world. The PGA Tour could teach us some of the following lessons.

The PGA Tour is not just about golf; it also offers valuable insights into leadership, teamwork, and strategic decision-making. By exploring the PGA Tour, you can draw parallels between the strategies employed by golfers and those used in the business world. This chapter can provide valuable lessons for those of you who are interested in leadership and management.

The PGA Tour is a platform where golfers strive for success and achievement. By highlighting the stories of successful golfers, their journey to the top, and the challenges they faced along the way, I hope to inspire you to strive for excellence in your business endeavors. PGA Tour golf professionals have inspiring stories of success, perseverance, and overcoming challenges on their journey to the top. Here are a few notable stories.

Tiger Woods is one of the most successful and well-known golfers in history. He turned professional in 1996 and quickly rose to the top of the golfing world. Woods faced numerous challenges, including injuries and personal setbacks, but he consistently demonstrated resilience and determination. Despite his struggles, he continued to work hard, refine his skills, and regain his form. His dedication paid off as he achieved a remarkable comeback by winning the 2019 Masters Tournament, after a gap of eleven years since his last major victory. Tiger Woods' story inspires individuals to never give up, even in the face of adversity, and to continually strive for greatness in their endeavors. Tiger Woods faced several challenges throughout his career. One significant challenge was injuries. Woods experienced multiple injuries, including knee surgeries and back problems, which affected his performance and required him to take breaks from the game. These injuries not only impacted his physical abilities but also tested his mental resilience. Additionally, Woods faced personal challenges in his personal life, including a highly publicized scandal and subsequent divorce, which had a profound impact on his career and public image. Despite these setbacks, Woods demonstrated determination, perseverance, and a strong work ethic to overcome these challenges and make a successful comeback.

Phil Mickelson is known for his aggressive and fearless playing style, Mickelson has won multiple major championships and is considered one of the greatest left-handed golfers of all time. Throughout his career, Mickelson faced the challenge of competing against other talented golfers, including Tiger Woods. Despite being in Woods' shadow, Mickelson persevered, constantly improving his game and challenging himself to reach new heights. His determination and commitment to excellence serve as an inspiration to individuals striving to excel in their business endeavors by never settling for mediocrity and continuously pushing their boundaries.

Phil Mickelson's playing style, characterized by his aggressive and fearless approach, has contributed to his success in several ways. Mickelson's willingness to take risks and attempt challenging shots has allowed him to make bold and decisive moves on the golf course. This playing style has often resulted in spectacular shots and memorable victories. While it may lead to occasional mistakes or setbacks, Mickelson's confidence and willingness to take calculated risks have also led to numerous triumphs. His playing style reflects his belief in his abilities and his commitment to pushing the boundaries of his game, which has contributed to his success as a golfer.

Arnold Palmer, often referred to as "The King," is a legendary figure in golf. He won numerous tournaments and played a significant role in popularizing the sport. Palmer's story is one of humble beginnings and hard work. He grew up in a small town and faced financial challenges, but his love for golf and determination to succeed propelled him forward. Palmer's charisma, sportsmanship, and connection with fans made him a beloved figure in the sport. His story inspires individuals to embrace their passion, work hard, and maintain a positive and engaging attitude, even in the face of adversity.

Annika Sörenstam is a Swedish professional golfer who achieved great success on the LPGA Tour. Sörenstam's journey to the top was marked by hard work, discipline, and breaking barriers. She faced challenges as a female golfer in a male-dominated sport but persevered and became one of the most dominant players in women's golf. Sörenstam's dedication to her craft, focus on continuous improvement, and relentless pursuit of excellence serve as a source of inspiration for individuals striving to succeed in their business endeavors, especially in industries where they may be underrepresented or face obstacles.

As a female golfer, Annika Sörenstam faced several obstacles. One significant challenge was the gender disparity and the lack of opportunities for women in professional golf. At the time when Sörenstam entered the sport, women's golf did not receive as much recognition or financial support as men's golf. Sörenstam had to confront stereotypes and biases that questioned the ability of women to compete at the highest level of the sport. However, she shattered these barriers through her exceptional performance and determination. Sörenstam's success and dominance in women's golf not only earned her respect but also helped pave the way for future generations of female golfers. Her achievements continue to inspire women in golf and in other industries, demonstrating that with talent, hard work, and perseverance, one can overcome gender-based obstacles and achieve greatness.

These stories of successful PGA Tour professionals highlight the importance of resilience, determination, continuous improvement, and a passion for one's craft. They inspire individuals to embrace challenges, overcome setbacks, and strive for excellence in their business endeavors. By learning from these golfers' stories, individuals can find motivation and guidance to pursue their goals, push beyond their limits, and achieve success in their chosen fields.

The PGA Tour brings together players, sponsors, industry professionals, and fans in a shared environment. Golfers have the chance to interact and network with fellow players, sponsors, and other influential individuals in the golf industry. This networking can lead to collaborations, mentorship opportunities, and even potential business ventures outside of golf.

The importance of networking and relationship building in both golf and business cannot be overstated. In golf, building connections with fellow players can lead to practice partnerships, friendly rivalries that push each other to improve, and even teaming up for tournaments or charity events. For example, professional golfers often form partnerships for team events like the Ryder Cup or Presidents Cup, where they work together to represent their respective countries. These relationships can provide support, motivation, and opportunities for growth within the sport.

Similarly, in business, networking and relationship building are crucial for career growth and business success. Meaningful connections with industry professionals can open doors to new opportunities, mentorship, and collaboration. For instance, a golfer who has built strong relationships with sponsors and industry professionals may have access to investment opportunities or business ventures related to golf course development, equipment manufacturing, or sports management.

Networking and relationship building play a vital role in both golf and business. The PGA Tour provides opportunities for golfers to connect with sponsors, fellow players, and industry professionals, which can lead to career growth and business success. Building meaningful connections can open doors to collaborations, mentorship, investment opportunities, and various ventures both within and outside of the golf industry. PGA Tour golf professionals have inspiring stories of success, perseverance, and overcoming challenges on their journey to the top. Here are a few notable stories.

The PGA Tour is known for its branding and marketing strategies, which can be analyzed and applied to the business world. By examining how the PGA Tour has built its brand and engaged with fans, you can provide insights into effective branding and marketing techniques that can be adapted to businesses of all sizes.

This chapter offers real-life examples, anecdotes, and practical insights that bridge the gap between golf and business. It provides you with a good understanding of the parallels between the two worlds and inspires you to apply the lessons learned to your professional lives.

Also, the PGA Tour offers valuable lessons for readers interested in leadership and management. By examining the organization's leadership practices and management strategies, you can gain insights into effective ways to navigate the business world. Here are some key insights that can be derived from the PGA Tour.

Goal Setting and Strategy

The PGA Tour is driven by a clear goal, which is to provide a platform for professional golfers to compete at the highest level. The organization's strategic planning and execution are evident in their tournament schedules, player rankings, and sponsorship agreements. By studying the PGA Tour's approach to goal setting and strategy, you can learn the importance of setting clear objectives, developing a strategic plan, and effectively executing it.

Adaptability and Resilience

Golfers on the PGA Tour face various challenges, including unpredictable weather conditions, tough competition, and the need to constantly adapt to different courses. The ability to adapt and remain resilient is crucial for success in both golf and business. By examining how PGA Tour professionals handle adversity, readers can gain insights into the importance of adaptability, perseverance, and maintaining a positive mindset in the face of challenges.

Teamwork and Collaboration

While golf is often seen as an individual sport, the PGA Tour also emphasizes the importance of teamwork and collaboration. Golfers work closely with their caddies, coaches, and support staff to optimize their performance. Furthermore, the PGA Tour itself operates as a team, with various departments working together to organize and execute tournaments. By studying the PGA Tour's emphasis on teamwork and collaboration, you can learn the value of building strong relationships, fostering collaboration, and leveraging the expertise of others to achieve collective success.

Examining the branding and marketing strategies of the PGA Tour can also provide you with valuable insights. Here are a few key takeaways.

Building a Strong Brand

The PGA Tour has successfully built a strong brand that

is recognized worldwide. By analyzing their branding efforts, you can learn about the importance of consistent messaging, visual identity, and brand differentiation. Understanding how the PGA Tour has established itself as a premier golf organization can inspire readers to develop their strong and recognizable brands in the business world.

Engaging with Fans and Sponsors

The PGA Tour excels in engaging with its fans and sponsors through various channels, including social media, televised events, and interactive experiences. By examining their marketing strategies, you can gain insights into effective ways to engage with customers and create meaningful connections. The PGA Tour's ability to cultivate a passionate and loyal fan base can serve as a valuable lesson for businesses looking to build strong customer relationships.

Leveraging Partnerships

The PGA Tour has successfully formed partnerships with various sponsors, broadcasters, and charitable organizations. By studying these partnerships, you can learn about the benefits of collaboration and how to leverage strategic alliances for mutual growth and impact. The PGA Tour's ability to create win-win partnerships can inspire you to seek out and nurture strategic relationships in your business endeavors.

Overall, examining the leadership and management practices of the PGA Tour provides valuable lessons in goal setting, adaptability, teamwork, and collaboration. Analyzing the branding and marketing strategies of the PGA Tour offers insights into building a strong brand, engaging with stakeholders, and leveraging partnerships. These insights can be applied to the business world, helping you enhance your leadership skills and develop effective strategies for success.

You can learn valuable lessons from the PGA Tour's approach to goal setting and strategy. The PGA Tour's focus on setting clear objectives and developing a strategic plan can be applied to the world of trading. You can benefit from the following insights.

Setting Clear Goals

The PGA Tour sets clear goals for its players, such as winning tournaments, earning a spot in the FedExCup playoffs, or qualifying for major championships. Similarly, traders can set specific, measurable, achievable, relevant, and time-bound (SMART) goals. For example, a trader may set a goal to achieve a certain percentage of return on investment within a specific timeframe. By setting clear goals, traders can stay focused and motivated.

Developing a Strategic Plan

The PGA Tour strategically plans its tournament schedules, taking into account factors such as player availability, course conditions, and fan engagement. Traders can learn from this approach by developing a strategic plan that includes factors such as market analysis, risk management strategies, and target opportunities. By having a well-defined plan, traders can make informed decisions and increase their chances of success.

Adapting to Changing Conditions

Golfers on the PGA Tour constantly adapt to changing conditions, such as weather changes, course challenges, and competitor performance. Similarly, traders need to be adaptable and flexible in response to market fluctuations and changing economic conditions. By studying how PGA Tour professionals adapt their strategies to different circumstances, traders can learn to adjust their trading approaches to optimize their performance.

Examining how PGA Tour professionals handle adversity can provide valuable insights for you. Here are a few examples.

Maintaining a Positive Mindset

PGA Tour professionals face challenges such as bad shots, missed putts, and pressure-filled situations. However, they often demonstrate resilience and maintain a positive mindset. You can learn from this by developing mental resilience and not letting setbacks or losses impact your overall trading performance. By staying positive and focused, you can navigate through challenging market conditions and maintain confidence in your business strategies.

Learning from Failures

The PGA Tour emphasizes teamwork and collaboration, despite being an individual sport. Here are a few examples.

Caddie Relationship

Golfers on the PGA Tour work closely with their caddies, who provide guidance, advice, and support during tournaments. The player-caddie relationship is built on trust, communication, and collaboration. You can learn from this by recognizing the importance of having a support system, such as mentors, colleagues, or trading communities, who can provide guidance and feedback. Collaborating with others can enhance decision-making and lead to better outcomes.

Organizational Collaboration

The PGA Tour operates as a team, with various departments working together to organize and execute tournaments. From tournament operations to marketing and media relations, each department collaborates to create a seamless experience for players, sponsors, and fans. You can gain insights from this approach by recognizing the value of collaboration with different stakeholders in the business. Collaborative efforts can lead to access to valuable resources, information sharing, and potential partnerships.

By examining the PGA Tour's emphasis on goal setting, strategy, handling adversity, teamwork, and collaboration, you can gain valuable insights to enhance your business practices. Applying these lessons can help you set clear goals, develop strategic plans, adapt to market conditions, maintain a positive mindset, learn from failures, and collaborate effectively with others.

Setting SMART goals is crucial for business owners to create, implement, and enforce effective strategies. SMART goals are specific, measurable, achievable, relevant, and time-bound. Here's how business owners can develop SMART goals.

Specific: Goals should be clearly defined and specific. For example, instead of setting a vague goal like "increase sales," a business owner can set a specific goal such as "increase monthly sales by 10 percent."

Measurable: Goals should have measurable criteria to track progress and success. For example, a business owner can measure the goal of increasing sales by tracking the revenue generated each month.

Achievable: Goals should be realistic and achievable. Business owners should consider their resources, capabilities, and market conditions when setting goals. Setting unrealistic goals can lead to frustration and demotivation.

Relevant: Goals should be relevant to the business's overall objectives and align with its mission and vision. For example, a goal to expand into a new market should be relevant to the business's long-term growth strategy.

Time-Bound: Goals should have a specific timeframe for completion. This helps create a sense of urgency and accountability. For example, a business owner can set a goal to increase social media followers by 20 percent within six months.

In addition to setting SMART goals, business owners should develop a strategic plan that incorporates market analysis and risk management strategies. Here's how you can do it.

Market Analysis

Business owners should conduct thorough market analysis to understand their target market, customer needs, and competitor landscape. This analysis helps identify market trends, opportunities, and potential threats. By gathering market insights, business owners can make informed decisions and develop strategies that resonate with their target audience.

Risk Management Strategies

Business owners should assess and mitigate potential risks that may impact their business. This includes identifying financial risks, operational risks, legal risks, and external factors such as economic fluctuations or industry disruptions. By developing risk management strategies, business owners can minimize the negative impact of potential risks and ensure business continuity.

Business owners can learn valuable lessons from how PGA Tour professionals adapt their strategies to different circumstances. Here are a few examples.

Course Conditions

PGA Tour professionals adapt their strategies based on the condition of the golf course. For example, if the course is wet and the ball doesn't roll as far, golfers may adjust their club selection and approach shots differently. Similarly, business owners can learn to adapt their strategies based on external factors such as changing market conditions, customer preferences, or technological advancements.

Competitor Performance

PGA Tour professionals closely monitor the performance of their competitors and adjust their strategies accordingly. If a competitor is consistently outperforming others, golfers may analyze their playing style and make adjustments to stay competitive. Business owners can apply this approach by regularly monitoring their competitors' activities, analyzing their strengths and weaknesses, and adapting their strategies to gain a competitive edge.

Personal Performance

PGA Tour professionals assess their performance and improve their game. They may analyze their swing, putting technique, or mental approach to identify areas for improvement. Similarly, business owners can evaluate their performance, identify areas for growth, and adapt their strategies to enhance their business operations, leadership, or customer experience.

Set Timeframes

Assigning a time frame to goals adds measurability. For instance, the business owner can set a goal to achieve a specific revenue target within a certain period, like "increase revenue by 10 percent within the next quarter."

It is important for goals to be achievable and relevant to a business for several reasons including.

Motivation and Focus

Setting achievable goals provides a sense of motivation and focus for business owners and their teams. Unrealistic goals may lead to frustration and demotivation, whereas achievable goals inspire action and a sense of accomplishment.

Resource Allocation

Goals that are relevant to a business's objectives ensure efficient allocation of resources. By aligning goals with the overall business strategy, owners can prioritize investments, manpower, and time in areas that contribute to the desired outcomes.

Strategic Decision-Making

Relevant goals guide strategic decision-making. They help business owners make informed choices about product development, marketing strategies, customer targeting, and resource allocation, leading to more effective and impactful decisions.

Performance Evaluation

PGA Tour professionals constantly evaluate their performance and improve. They analyze their swing, putting technique, and mental approach to identify areas of growth. Similarly, business owners can evaluate their performance, identify strengths and weaknesses, and adapt their strategies to enhance their operations and achieve better results.

By developing specific and measurable goals, ensuring their achievability and relevance to the business, and learning from PGA Tour professionals' adaptability, business owners can drive growth, stay competitive, and navigate through changing circumstances.

CHAPTER 13:
CONCLUSION: THE DEFINITION OF SUCCESS

"To do more for the world than the World does for you — that is success."

– Henry Ford

It is my fervent desire that you have enjoyed reading this book and that you will apply some of the ideas mentioned herewith such as goal setting, consistency, building a strong team, firing fast and hiring slow, measuring performance, learning how your mental and emotional factors affect your performance, reviewing the qualities that are important for achieving and maintaining success, observing why some golf players and business owners fail, and concluding the importance of taking the right action.

When Henry Ford said, "To do more for the world than the world does for you," he was expressing the idea of contributing and making a positive impact on the world rather than solely focusing on personal gains. This quote reflects Ford's belief in the importance of service, giving back, and leaving a legacy.

1. **Going Beyond Self-Interest:** A successful person thinks beyond their needs and desires. Instead of solely pursuing personal success or benefit, he suggests that one should strive to make a difference in the world. It emphasizes the idea that true

fulfillment and purpose come from contributing to the greater good.

2. **Making a Positive Impact:** Ford's quote implies that one should aim to make a positive difference in the world. Whether it's through innovation, philanthropy, social activism, or any other means, the focus is on using one's abilities and resources to improve the lives of others and society.

3. **Challenging the Status Quo:** By suggesting that individuals should do more for the world, Ford implies that the world may not always provide everything we desire or expect. It encourages people to take initiative, be proactive, and challenge conventional norms or expectations to create positive change.

4. **Leaving a Legacy:** Ford's quote also suggests that our actions should have a lasting impact. It emphasizes the importance of leaving the world in a better state than we found it. It encourages individuals to think long-term and consider how their contributions can have a ripple effect beyond their immediate sphere of influence.

Overall, Henry Ford's quote serves as a reminder to prioritize service, contribution, and making a positive impact on the world. It encourages individuals to think beyond personal gains and consider how they can leave a legacy of meaningful change.

In my opinion, the definition of success for a successful golfer and/or a successful business owner may differ, but both can contribute to the well-being of their community.

For any golfer, much like a business person, success is often measured by their performance and achievements. It can include winning tournaments, achieving high rankings, improving their skills, and reaching personal goals. Success for a golfer is often tied to their individual performance and the recognition they receive within the golfing community.

On the other hand, success for a business owner is often

measured by the growth and profitability of their business. It includes factors such as increasing revenue, expanding market share, building a strong brand, and creating a positive impact on the industry. Success for a business owner is often tied to the overall success and sustainability of their business.

While the definitions of success may vary, both golfers and business owners can contribute to the well-being of their community.

Economic Impact

Successful golfers and business owners can contribute to the economic well-being of their community by generating revenue and creating job opportunities. Golf tournaments and events hosted by successful golfers can attract visitors and tourists, boosting local businesses such as hotels, restaurants, and retail establishments. Similarly, successful business owners can create employment opportunities and stimulate economic growth within their community.

Philanthropy and Giving Back

Both golfers and business owners can give back to their community through philanthropic initiatives. They can use their success and resources to support charitable causes, sponsor community events, donate to local organizations, or establish foundations that address social or environmental issues. By investing in their community, they can make a positive impact and improve the well-being of those around them.

Role Models and Inspiration

Successful golfers and business owners can serve as role models and inspire others in their community. Their achievements and success stories can motivate aspiring golfers or entrepreneurs to pursue their goals and dreams. They can share their knowledge, experiences, and mentorship to help others succeed and contribute to the growth and development of their community.

Community Engagement

Golfers and business owners can actively engage with their community through various initiatives. They can participate in local events, sponsor sports programs or business development activities, and collaborate with community organizations or schools. By actively engaging with the community, they can build relationships, foster a sense of belonging, and contribute to the overall well-being of their community.

While your definition of success may differ, your achievements can significantly contribute to the well-being of your community. By making economic contributions, engaging in philanthropy, serving as a role model, and actively participating in community activities, you can make a positive impact. Leveraging your success and resources allows you to create a lasting and meaningful difference, fostering a thriving and supportive environment for those around you.

Success, whether on the golf course or in the business world, is often a journey marked by determination, clear goals, and a passion for what you do. My recent experience at the LPGA West Palm Beach Chapter's Pink Ball fundraising event perfectly encapsulates this journey. It was an event that brought together my love for golf, my thriving real estate business, and my passion for philanthropic endeavors. Recently, on a beautiful sunny morning, I found myself at the Pink Ball annual event at the Little Club in Delray Beach, Florida, playing golf with friends and colleagues. The Pink Ball event was more than just a game; it was a celebration and a fundraiser to support younger golfers aspiring to achieve their dreams. As we teed off, the camaraderie and friendly competition filled the air with electric energy, enthusiasm, and high expectations.

The day was meticulously planned, featuring not only the golf tournament but also a delightful fashion show, where I had the pleasure of modeling ladies' golf attire. The fusion of style and sport was a testament to the multifaceted nature of our passions and how they can be harmoniously intertwined. We enjoyed a sumptuous lunch, engaged in lively conversations, and celebrated each other's achievements with numerous prizes, including copies of my four published books.

This event was also a golden opportunity for me to promote my real estate business. Golf has always been a powerful networking tool, and this day was no exception. Engaging with fellow golfers, sharing insights about the market, and showcasing my latest listings seamlessly integrated business with pleasure. The genuine connections made on the golf course often translate into lasting professional relationships and successful deals.

Reflecting on this day, I realize how vital it is to have clear goals and expectations. Golf, much like business, requires focus, strategy, and a positive mindset. These principles have guided me throughout my career, helping me navigate challenges and celebrate successes.

As I look back, I see a life filled with purpose and joy, surrounded by supportive friends and colleagues. The blend of playing golf, promoting my business, and enjoying the finer aspects of life like fashion and good company, brings a sense of fulfillment that is truly priceless. It's a reminder that success is not just about financial gains but about living a balanced, joyous life where your passions fuel your achievements.

This book is not just the culmination of my experiences but also a testament to the power of combining passion with professionalism, proving that with clear goals and a positive outlook, one can achieve success both on the golf course and in the business world. As you turn to the final pages of this book, you have not only gained valuable insights but also experienced a profound transformation in your approach to both business and life. Through the stories and lessons shared, I aim to have equipped you with the mental resilience to face challenges head-on, the strategic foresight to set and achieve ambitious goals, and the adaptability to navigate an ever-changing landscape. You now recognize the importance of maintaining focus amidst distractions and understand the power of a positive mindset in overcoming obstacles. May you emerge from this journey with renewed confidence and a clear vision for your future endeavors, ready to turn your dreams into reality. Thank you for joining me on this path of growth and discovery.

Now, go score a hole-in-one!

ACKNOWLEDGMENTS

As I reflect on over five decades of my mission, my heart overflows with gratitude for the incredible individuals who have accompanied me on this journey. I wish to express my deepest thanks to my family and all those who have shared their precious time and energy with me.

The mission of this book is to serve those dear souls who will read it. I am profoundly grateful for the grace that has guided this entire process, and to the friends and teachers along my path – too many to mention, some renowned and others unsung – whose insights, strategies, love, and care are the shoulders I am honored to stand upon.

On this day, I extend my heartfelt thanks to you, the reader, and to all those I have had the privilege to meet, love, and serve.

ABOUT THE AUTHOR

Maria Ellis, MBA, is a graduate of the Harvard Business School Owner-President Management Program and earned her bachelor's degree in business administration as well as her MBA from the University of Massachusetts in Amherst. As a former international banker, investment advisor, and financial planner, Maria has specialized in converting clients' financial objectives into successful action plans. Maria has both the know-how and the market contacts, having worked at Bank of America, Citibank, the MONY Group, Northwestern Mutual, Citi Habitats and Keller Williams.

Maria is a Chopra Certified Health Instructor, and she is

the bestselling author of the Journey to Wellness, Freedom, and Legacy series, which includes *Achieve Financial Freedom: The Road Map to Financial Success*; *Family Business Legacy Plan: The Ultimate Guide to Creating a Legacy for Your Family without Paying too Much in Taxes*; *Redefining Entrepreneurial Success: A Guide to a Healthy and Holistic Lifestyle*; and *Longevity: Reinvent Yourself at Any Age.*

Maria's background includes board leadership positions at the College of Mount Saint Vincent, the American Association of University Women, and the Virginia Gildersleeve International Fund. Maria is also a pro-bono consultant at the Harvard Business School Club of New York City Community Partners and applies her business skills to a variety of topics, including strategic planning, marketing, finance, governance, and organizational development. Maria is an active member of the Harvard Club and the Genuis Network.

THANK YOU!

Thank you for reading my book about using the Tao of golf to achieve entrepreneurial success, which I wrote with you in mind. It is my earnest desire that you know how to navigate the world of business with the same ease as the pros do on the course, which is why I am offering you a complimentary consultation. To book your session, please email Maria Ellis at mellis@fsacap.com.

Made in United States
Cleveland, OH
22 January 2025

13680077R00085